DIE NIGGER DIE!

DIE NIGGER DIE!

A Political Autobiography
by H. Rap Brown

(Jamil Abdullah Al-Amin)

Foreword by Ekwueme Michael Thelwell

Lawrence Hill Books

Published by Lawrence Hill Books
An imprint of Chicago Review Press Incorporated
814 North Franklin Street
Chicago, Illinois 60610
ISBN 978-1-55652-452-3

This paperback edition of *Die Nigger Die!* is an unabridged republication
of the edition published in New York in 1969, and is reprinted by
arrangement with the author.

The lines from "Dream Deferred" by Langston Hughes, copyright 1951
by Langston Hughes, are reprinted from *The Panther and the Lash* by
permission of Alfred A. Knopf, Inc.

"Conquest" by Georgia Douglas Johnson is reprinted by permission of
Henry Lincoln Johnson. Published in *American Negro Poetry* edited by
Arna Bontemps, Hill and Wang, Inc.

The poem on page xli is reprinted with the kind permission of the author,
Don H. Lee.

Photographic material used in collages on pages 5, 6, 49, 50, 70, 71, 122,
123, 126, and 127 courtesy of Wide World Photos, Inc.

Printed in the United States of America

To
all of those who have died
resisting america's white death
and to
Murphy Bell
William Kunstler
Howard Moore

Foreword

H. Rap Brown/Jamil Al-Amin: A Profoundly American Story

This autobiographical political memoir by H. Rap Brown is a vital American historical document—historical almost in the sense of a message found in a time capsule, a missive from another age. But it remains of considerable interest for what it tells us about social and political attitudes, behaviors, and expectations of a time—so my students believe—long past. The time, in this case, is a discrete, relatively short period of domestic upheaval in this country during the late 1960s and early 1970s, a time of "revolutionary" black uprising in northern ghettoes following hard on the heels of the southern, nonviolent direct action movement engineered by SNCC (Student Nonviolent Coordinating Committee), CORE (Congress of Racial Equality), and SCLC (Southern Christian Leadership Conference), a movement usually associated with Martin Luther King, Jr. Rap's book has an added dimension of sociological interest, being a voice from the front lines, the personal and political testimony of a radically militant chairman of SNCC who came to symbolize the defiance of a generation of angry and militant black youth. A third, perhaps less compelling, area of interest is the personal: what the voice and language reveal about the character and personality, the sensibility, if you will, of the speaker. In combination these three factors make a powerful argument for the reissuing of this book. *Die Nigger Die!* is a cultural artifact that should be generally available.

So you would expect that the author, like any writer, would be immeasurably eager to see his work once more in print. But you would be wrong.

For one thing, the author, H. Rap Brown, is no longer among us. Nor has he really been since 1971, when, as a young man of twenty-six, he made his *shahadah* (the Muslim declaration of faith). During a period of incarceration by the State of New York, the black activist known to the media as H. Rap Brown converted to orthodox Islam and emerged as Jamil Abdullah Al-Amin, a Sunni Muslim. Brown went in and Al-Amin emerged. This change was by no means cosmetic or strategic.

By all accounts and the overwhelming preponderance of evidence over many years, this was a genuine religious conversion, a classically "profound transformation of self." Al-Amin embarked on a life of rigorous study and spiritual and moral inquiry with the same single-minded intensity and uncompromising commitment Rap had brought to militant social struggle.

It is important to mention this because, as we know, not all conversions—religious or ideological—are equal. This was a time particularly famous for instant sudden, public, and apparently infinitely reversible self-reinventions, two of the more dramatic being Jerry Rubin's conversion from the stridently counterculture Youth International Party leadership to Wall Street broker (from yippie to yuppie) and Eldridge Cleaver's from Black Panther Party revolutionary to born-again Christian.

Al-Amin's embrace of Islam, however, proved neither facile nor expedient, as his emergence as a bookish Muslim cleric and his years of work in faith-based social improvement have demonstrated. The fiery and impetuous young rebel who speaks out of the pages of this book has long since evolved into an austere religious scholar, disciplined by faith and projecting the aura of a spiritually disposed ascetic.

After thirty years, Al-Amin has become, in many important ways, a vastly different person from the author of this book. A respected Imam, he now sees—and for some time has seen—the world, his own role therein, and the eventual liberation of his people in quite different terms: those of faith, self-discipline, and spiritual development. This vision is reflected in both his demeanor and his language. Consequently he has, at this time, serious reservations about the appropriateness of reissuing this book of youthful struggle. It is not that he repudiates any aspect of the earlier book— not the tone, the defiant struggle out of which it came, or even the youthful persona of that text. (The Imam, however, did have some concerns whether the vernacular earthiness of some of the street language was now entirely seemly. He also found a number of pejorative street-corner references to certain women to be regrettable, even embarrassing, but decided to let them stand as originally uttered.)

His reservation is more that he considers his more recent work, *Revolution by the Book*, far more relevant to his current concerns and the work of thirty years, as well as being more indicative of his present personal and professional style. No two books could be more different in style and subject, but what they share, apart from their common paternity, is that both are earnestly addressed to the same audience and purpose: the re-education of the African American grassroots.

This more recent work is not, as might be inferred from a casual glance at the title, a handbook on guerrilla war. The revolution of the title refers very specifically to jihad in its classical Islamic meaning of the daily internal struggle for self-mastery and moral discipline. The book begins with a collection of sermons, each explicating one of the Five Pillars of Islam—*Shahadah* (declaration of faith), *Tauheed* (the Oneness and uniqueness of God), *Salaat* (prayer and worship), *Zakaat* (the redemptive value of charity), and *Saum* (purification by fasting and abstinence)—and the expression of all five by the *Hajj*, or prescribed pilgrimage.

Liberally illustrated with quotations from the Qur'an, the *Sunnah*, and other secondary Islamic texts, the tone is learned and reverent, exhortatory and precise. It is an eloquent articulation of the fundamental principles, values, and practice of orthodox Islam, affecting every aspect of life, personal and social. The revolution it envisions is a moral one, which begins with the personal, stressing awareness of God and self through piety, study, and self-discipline, and moves through family and out into the larger society.

On family:

The first responsibility of the Muslim is as teacher. That is his job, to teach. His first school, his first classroom is within the household. His first student is himself. He masters himself and then he begins to convey the knowledge that he has acquired to the family. The people who are closest to him.

On struggle:

To be successful in struggle requires remembrance of the Creator and the doing of good deeds. This is important because successful struggle demands that there be a kind of social consciousness. There has to be a social commitment, a social consciousness that joins men together. On the basis of their coming together, they do not transgress against themselves and they do not transgress against others.

On society and revolution:

When you understand your obligations to God then you can understand your obligations to society. Revolution comes when human beings set out to correct decadent institutions. We must understand how this society has fallen away from righteousness and begin to develop, Islamically, the alternative institutions to those that are in a state of decline around us. But we must first enjoin right and forbid wrong to ourselves. That is the first step in turning this thing around: turn your self around.

There is a directness and, if you will, a sincerity to this language, a sincerity that those who know the Imam say has for thirty years been evident in the man's life and example. These qualities are said to have earned him a fierce loyalty and affection from the Muslim congregation to which he ministers in a working-class suburb of Atlanta, respect in the surrounding Christian neighborhood, and a wider regard in the national Muslim-American community. This side of Al-Amin's vocational persona is one I had not been privileged to observe until quite recently.

This was in 1998 at a farewell tribute to our brother Kwame Ture (Stokely Carmichael), who was stricken with terminal cancer and about to leave for Africa, there to die. Perhaps two thousand people had gathered in the banquet room of a Washington hotel: family, friends, admirers, and supporters of Carmichael's, mostly movement faithful, veterans of the "heroic days."

It would have been a remarkable gathering in any place and any decade, though it could probably not have happened in the 1960s, when doctrinal and ideological disagreement had loomed so urgent and divisive. Even recently, perhaps only respect for Carmichael could have assembled such a gathering. Next to each other were Black Nationalists and Southern Baptists; pan-Africanists, native Africans, a few Sunni Muslims, and NAACP integrationists next to Nation of Islam separatists; former Black Panthers next to former Students for a Democratic Society activists; progressive intellectuals—writers and editors—Socialists, Marxists, liberals, black and white, next to Black Arts Movement cultural nationalists; and John Lewis, the majority whip of the U.S. House of Representatives, cheek by jowl with Minister Louis Farrakhan, the ubiquitous leader of the Nation of Islam. It was a fitting tribute to the extraordinary range and reach of Carmichael/Ture's political and personal charisma and the affection he commanded across lines of ideology and identity.

Prominent at the speakers' table were the former chairmen of the Student Nonviolent Coordinating Committee (Marion Barry, Chuck McDew, John Lewis, Jamil, and Phil Hutchens). The talk from the platform was, as might be expected, nostalgic, affectionate, political. The only real departure and my only surprise came when Imam Al-Amin spoke. What he delivered in tribute to his old friend was a thoughtful, Islam-inflected reflection on the nature of oppression and the moral duty, the religious imperative, of the faithful to resist. Liberally adorned with qur'anic quotations, it was, as I recall, an erudite, elegantly constructed, finely reasoned explication of the categories and nature of oppression and the moral dimensions and complexities of struggle as expressed in the prophetic poetry of the Arabian desert some fourteen hundred years earlier. In any terms—culturally speaking—it was scholarly. I found it startling in a curious way: it did not quite fit either stylistically or culturally with what had gone before, yet was completely appropriate.

Its traditional opening in the resonant cadences of classic Arabic poetry—"Al-landu lillah; Al-hamdu lillahi; rabb-il aalameen; bismi-llah-ir-rahman-ir-rahim. . ."* —seemed to me and others a voice and sensibility out of a different culture and another time. Its text, taken from Sura 42, verse 41 of the Holy Qur'an— "All those who fight when oppressed incur no guilt, but Allah shall surely perish the oppressor"—seemed appropriate as a personal credo both for the speaker and for the life of struggle being recognized.

As he spoke, I remember thinking: Ah, so *this* is what a serious Islamic sermon sounds like, huh? Rap really takes this

---

* "Praise belongs to God. All praise belongs to God, Lord of the Worlds. In the name of God, the Beneficent, the Merciful. . ."

calling seriously. The brother is indeed an Islamic scholar, an Imam. (I took the long-jawed look of astonishment and professional respect that crossed Minister Farrakhan's face as he listened to be confirmation of my impression.)

I'd known the youthful Rap at Howard University as the younger brother of my friend Ed, and, of course, later with SNCC in Mississippi and Alabama, before he erupted in the nation's headlines as the black militant from Hell, the Negro America loved to hate. I remembered a laconic, rangy (six-foot-five), hawk-faced youth, mostly silent, a preternaturally watchful, almost brooding presence. Said to be an extraordinary athlete, he looked the part.

"Yeah, the boy can play him some ball, Bro. Everything from point guard to power forward and some quarterback too," his brother told me. "An' there ain't no dawg in mah boy either. He a competitor from his heart. No quit in him."

Given the times, it was natural that the movement would draw him away from the courts and the possibility of athletic scholarships. He listened to our endless debates, read voraciously, joined our demonstrations, and volunteered for the Mississippi Summer Project of 1964. In 1965 he was back in D.C., where he became chairman of NAG (Nonviolent Action Group), the local SNCC affiliate. This led to the infamous White House confrontation with President Lyndon B. Johnson (see pp. 51–53).

I believe it was a Saturday morning a week following the vicious police riot known as "Bloody Sunday" on the Elmer Pettus Bridge in Selma, Alabama. I was alone in the SNCC office when the telephone rang from the Leadership Conference on Civil Rights. Responding to international outrage over the atrocity in Alabama, President Johnson had suddenly agreed to a meeting with the Civil Rights leadership. However, the meeting was that afternoon and the leadership was scattered all over the country. The Washington representatives would have to stand in. Would I be representing SNCC? Hell, no, I most certainly would not. Just then in strolls Rap, attired, as I recall, for athletic endeavor.

"Hey, aren't you the chairman of NAG? Feel like going to the White House this afternoon?" Rap considered it for several moments.

"Well," he drawled, "why not? I ain't really doing much this afternoon."

Later, when he gave his report, I remember his indignation and amazement at the fawning subservience toward the President displayed by a delegation ostensibly there to represent the urgency of our people's struggle, courtiers so effusively grateful for the privilege merely of being there and so anxious to preserve their access that none dared be forthright with the monarch. So it had fallen to him to raise the questions of presidential responsibility for federal inaction in protecting the rights of black citizens that the group was there to represent. He described the delegation's shuffling during the meeting and their not-very-subtle distancing of themselves from his intemperance, in some cases even going so far as to apologize for him. Yet once outside they effusively praised his courage for saying the things that "needed to be said." Then, within the week, an insidious column in the *Washington Post* (Evans and Novak) described how "deeply embarrassed responsible Civil Rights leaders" were professing to be at the "disrespect" shown the President by the young student.

(Rap told me that LBJ had entered the meeting expressing his great displeasure at all-night demonstrations outside the White House, which were so noisy that "his little girls" had been unable to sleep. The courtiers each in their turn had expressed distress and apologies for this inconvenience to the presidential family. Rap, when his turn came, said that he too was real sad that for one night the presidential daughters' repose had been disturbed, but black people in the South had been unable to sleep in peace and security for a hundred years. What did the President plan to do about that? He had thought that this was what they were meeting to discuss. Which apparently so upset the President that the courtiers subsequently felt a need to run to the press to put their disapproval on the public record. It must have been a generational thing.)

When, in 1967 at the age of twenty-three, Rap succeeded Carmichael as SNCC chairman, it was at a tense and desperate moment in the country. SNCC's call for Black Power, coupled with its stand against the Vietnam War, had isolated the organization and left it exposed. Deep fissures had appeared in the Civil Rights "coalition." The long-simmering anger at racism and economic injustice of alienated black youth in the ghettoes was erupting into violent and destructive urban insurrections. In every case these "riots" were triggered by police brutality or misconduct, most usually the killing or brutalizing of an unarmed black man.

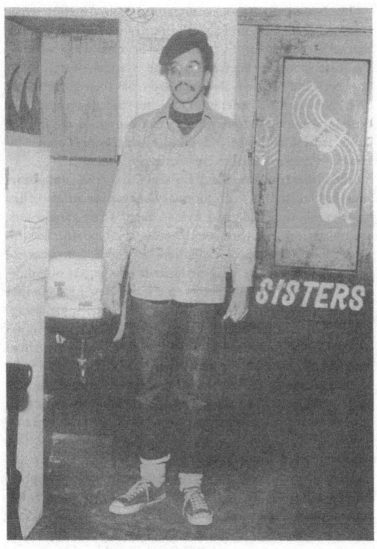

H. Rap Brown at Soulville, U.S.A., a club in New Orleans, circa 1968. Photograph by Marion Porter; from the collection of Eric Waters.

The black insurrections traumatized white America, which was further divided, usually along generational and class lines, by the Vietnam War. Suddenly, middle-class white youth—the ostensible beneficiaries of the system—were, to an unprecedented degree, also alienated from their government. The "New Left," a generation of white student activists, was becoming increasingly strident in its denouncement of the American establishment, adopting an increasingly anti-capitalist and anti-imperialist "revolutionary" rhetoric.

About this time, the Black Panther Party made its appearance in Oakland. A "revolutionary" organization of urban black youth, they had great style. A variation on gang colors, their black leather jackets, black berets, and blue shirts—with firearms either visible or implied—were an expression of ghetto youth culture. Appearing as if on cue out of America's Third World, the Panthers were the New Left's homegrown surrogates for the Viet Cong. Black, virile, menacing, hip guerrillas, the Panthers were—depending on one's orientation—the incarnation of white America's most primal fantasy or its worst nightmare: angry Negroes with guns.

Their leadership, with a well-developed sense of theater and an instinct for hustle, permitted the white New Left to declare them the revolutionary vanguard, with predictable results. Their members paid a terrible price: some were killed and many are still in jail, often on very dubious charges.

All of which, in the media's dependably sensationalist presentation, contributed mightily to a pervasive mood of racial tension and impending doom across the nation. Wars (abroad) and rumors of (race) war at home—mere anarchy is loosed, the center cannot hold? Something like that.

Well, not by a long shot, pilgrim. Not if J. Edgar Hoover and his FBI had anything to say, which they did. If brute force, illegality, and criminal anarchy were to be the order of the day (which was by no means clear), why, then, it were best it came from good ol' Uncle Sam himself, yes, indeed.

The Bureau's response, a "hard-hitting" national counter-intelligence program (COINTELPRO), was of surpassing ruthlessness in its contempt for law and the civil rights of the citizens. COINTELPRO cast a wide net covering the Peace Movement, the New Left, student activists, black militants ("Black nationalist hate groups"), and pacifist clergy, including even the very churchly Dr. Martin Luther King, Jr. The Director's specific instructions were to use all necessary means to "expose, disrupt, misdirect, discredit or otherwise neutralize . . . black nationalist hate type organizations [sic], their leadership, spokesmen, membership and supporters . . ." Programs designed to "convince them," the Director instructed his agents, *that to be a black revolutionary is to be a dead revolutionary.*"

The Bureau, taking him at his word, came up with a repertoire of dirty tricks—each authorized by the Director and usually illegal*—ranging from character assassination, disinformation, false arrest on bogus charges, manufactured evidence, perjured testimony, and cynical frame-ups to physical assassination by either uniformed officers or hired agents. All of this has been documented by Congressional investigation

---

* The order directing action against Dr. King instructed that "it may be unrealistic to limit our actions to legalistic proofs [*sic*] that would stand up in court or before Congressional committees."

and none of the perpetrators—the "rogue agents"—within the Bureau has ever served a day of jail time.

This being the context in which H. Rap Brown undertook the SNCC chairmanship, it is therefore not surprising that his term of office, a succession of indictments and arrests, was spent mostly in court, out on bond, or in jail. Some of this is recounted in this book.

It began in July 1967 after an appearance in Cambridge, Maryland, where he had given an "incendiary" and—in the presence of the media—politically ill-advised speech in which he urged black people to arm themselves, be "ready to die," and to meet violence with violence. "This town is ready to explode . . . if you don't have guns, don't be here . . . you have to be ready to die." This proved rather quickly prophetic: immediately after the speech he and two companions were fired on from an ambush, and the community exploded.

After I spoke people were just milling around. A young lady who lived up towards Race Street where a bunch of white policemen were gathered asked for an escort home because she was afraid to walk by herself. Myself and two other people were walking her home and some dudes opened fire on us with shotguns from some bushes. We found out later they [the shooters] were black policemen. They were shooting at us a long time. I was hit, I dove to the ground, rolled into a ditch and made my way into someone's yard.

After the shooting there was a lot of commotion. People went into the street and just started tearing everything up. A few hours later they burned the school again. Two weeks earlier people had burned the black elementary school because it had been a rat infested, roach infested place. People were paying taxes and their children were forced to go to school in those conditions. It is these conditions which cause riots. Not anybody's rhetoric. (H.R.B., 1992)

Shortly after this incident, Brown was charged by the State of Maryland with incitement to riot, beginning a succession of charges and protracted legal maneuvering drawn out over a two-year period.

I can remember following the process as it unfolded in an almost Kafkaesque absurdity in the press. It seemed like every few months he would be hauled into court in a new jurisdiction on a different charge and held under an oppressively large bond. His attorney—the late Bill Kunstler—would struggle mightily to win a reduction. Rap would eventually come out and in a matter of days be reported somewhere else making even more "incendiary" utterances and be back in custody, there to begin the dismal cycle all over again. At least that's how it seemed to me. I can remember saying, "I guess you're right. Rap don't have no quit in him after all, but maybe he should." And Ed growling, "That boy hard-headed, Bro. Jes' too damn stubborn."

Subsequently released FBI documents make it clear that this process of paralysis by indictment and legal intimidation was by no means limited to H. Rap Brown. It was a deliberate, across-the-board COINTELPRO strategy designed to cripple radical organizations by misusing the courts. First, arrests of targeted activists on serious charges carrying potentially long sentences. It was of little importance to the government whether or not they had a legitimate case strong enough to secure a conviction. The point was to silence and immobilize leadership while forcing groups to redirect energy and resources into raising funds, organizing legal defenses, and publicizing these cases. It was a government subversion of the American justice system resulting in drawn-out Soviet-style political show trials that became common-place in the America of the 1970s: the Chicago Seven, the Panther Twenty-One, etc., etc. Although the overwhelming majority of these cases did not result in convictions,* government documents show that they were considered great tactical successes. They kept the movements off the streets and in the courts.

However, a few convictions *were* attained, and it is clear that at least some activists who ended up serving long sentences—some of whom remain in jail to this day—were flat-out framed by their government. People were convicted on perjured testimony as witnesses were bribed or coerced into lying. Exculpatory evidence was withheld from the defense and made to "disappear." As I write, Leonard Peltier of the American Indian Movement is still in jail. Elmo "Geronimo" Pratt of the California Panthers, a decorated Vietnam veteran, was recently released after spending nearly half his life in jail for a murder *the FBI had clear evidence that he could not possibly have committed.* Similarly, Dhurubah Moore, a New York Panther, has only recently been freed after a review of his case indicated similar government misconduct. These are only a few cases that have surfaced into public awareness. But

---

* The Panther 21 is a case in point—twenty-one American citizens were arrested in coordinated, Gestapo-like pre-dawn raids in April 1969. It took almost two years, until May 1971, after the longest political trial in New York's history, before all were acquitted of *all* charges after all of forty-five minutes of jury deliberation. Public humiliation for the government? No, indeed. Privately, it was gleefully hailed as a great strategic victory. It had tied the New York Panthers up for two years, hadn't it?

there remain a great many such cases—some estimates say more than fifty—that seem irretrievably buried in the catacombs of legal bureaucracy. So that there are activists of that generation—fellow human beings and American citizens—in effect political prisoners *still* serving time in an American gulag, often on very questionable evidence indeed.

For instance, have you heard of the Angola Three? These are three black men in the Louisiana State Penitentiary—Herman Wallace, Robert Wilkenson, and Albert Woolfort—who have been held in continuous solitary confinement for twenty-eight years. These men are inmate activists responsible for organizing a functional chapter of the Black Panther Party among the inmate population of Angola. In 1972 the men were convicted of the murder of a guard and have been held in isolation ever since. It is now possible, and it is the duty of every thinking American, to take the opportunity to review the facts of these cases and the state's evidence on the basis of which these three men have been buried alive for nearly thirty years. (www.prisonactivist.org/angola)

Back to the Rap. In March 1970, after two years of tortuous legal jousting, he failed to appear in court for trial on the incitement charge and simply disappeared. For eighteen months, despite the best efforts of the FBI and an international dragnet, he appeared to have dropped from the face of the earth. To my knowledge he has never publicly discussed this period, so it remains something of a mystery. At the time, speculation was rife.

None of our mutual movement friends seemed to know—or would admit to knowing—his whereabouts. He was variously reported in Cuba, in Algeria, in West Africa, or deceased. His brother Ed was "pretty sure" he was alive, but so completely incommunicado that even he had not a clue as to where Rap might be.

When he finally surfaced in 1972 it was in truly astonishing circumstances and surprisingly close to home—midtown Manhattan, in fact. His friends and supporters in the movement were stunned when large *New York Times* headlines proclaimed his capture, gut-shot and seriously wounded, following a running gun battle with police during "an attempted hold-up" of an uptown Manhattan bar. To us this made no sense. Armed robbery of a bar? C'mon, that was completely at odds with the political principles we considered ourselves to share with Rap. And, besides, why would he, having successfully eluded capture for so long, now choose to chance so dubious, dangerous, and criminal an enterprise? It just simply made no sense. Indeed, had Rap not been in critical condition in a Harlem hospital, one would have been tempted to simply dismiss the entire story as false identification.

To many black Americans, this was an astonishing and dismaying development. The young SNCC chairman seemed to have crossed the line between militant political defiance and flat-out criminality. Some of the support he had enjoyed, both within the movement and in the general community, evaporated.

But by no means all. Some years afterward, the venerable and legendary New York Mookie, a retired player wise in the ways of the street, clued me in to the word. "It was some black nurses saved that boy's life, Prof." He nodded emphatically. "Yeah, them white doctors was goin' let the brother die, man. But they say it was some sisters from the islands, man, raised hell in that hospital. Took care of the brother.

Protected that boy. Made them doctors do what they s'posed to do. Yeah, Prof, it was them West Indian nurses saved that boy's life."

Another persistent story from the street, which Rap himself has never—at least not to me—confirmed nor denied, goes as follows: Some of his time underground was spent in a blighted Brooklyn community, an area ravaged by drugs. Along with some like-minded brothers, under arms, the fugitive ran those dealers out. Emboldened at having cleaned up one local community, they looked north. The bar in Manhattan was not just any bar. In close proximity to a police precinct, it was a favorite watering hole of some of New York's finest. It was also reputed to be the location where, once weekly, Harlem dealers gathered to settle accounts with their partners and protectors on the police force.

So, according to the street, the "stickup" was more accurately a punitive action intended to reinforce earlier warnings the dealers had ignored. If the law wouldn't stop them, then they would. A bad idea, poorly timed. In one version, the late shift at the precinct changed during the operation, bringing a new wave of armed, thirsty men into the bar. In another version, the crew simply walked into a carefully laid ambush. Whatever the case, the only ones who know for sure are, for their own good reasons, not about to talk, so H. Rap Brown's last public act went into the official record as an attempted armed robbery.

After recovering from his injuries, Rap served five years of a fifteen-year sentence. Having theoretically discharged his debt to the law, and re-emerged into society as Jamil Al-Amin, H. Rap Brown, for all intents and purposes, should have been history.

Paroled in 1976, Jamil Al-Amin, after making his *Hajj* to Mecca, settled in Atlanta, where his brother Ed was director of the Voter Education Project, and set out to construct a new life outside the glare of the media. A story from those times illustrates something of the ironies and difficulties attending attempts at anonymity by previously public figures.

The Johnson administration's response to urban unrest and the Kerner Commission's warning that "our nation is moving towards two societies, one black, one white, separate and unequal" was something called the National Urban Coalition. This initiative was intended to "save our cities" by mobilizing leadership of the public and private sectors to address the absence of viable educational and economic alternatives for minority youth, which was thought to be at the root of black alienation and anger. The argument was persuasive: people who have hope in their lives and a meaningful investment in their futures simply do not put the torch to their communities. Therefore the administration was calling for a national coalition at the highest level of corporate, philanthropic, religious, educational, and political leadership to mobilize the necessary resources—human and financial—to address the urban crisis. At the initial meeting McGeorge Bundy made the administration's pitch to a blue chip gathering of the American establishment.

At the end one "crusty old codger" allowed as how it seemed to make sense. But, dad-gummit, something about it just didn't sit quite right with him.

"And what might that be, sir?" Bundy asked.

"Well, Mr. Secretary, it just sounds to me like you're asking us to reward people for rioting, an' something about that just plain rubs me the wrong way." Murmurs of approval around the room. Not a penny for tribute?

"Well, sir, I can fully understand that," Bundy is reported to have said. "But let me put it to you this way . . . (thoughtful pause) . . . Wouldn't you, *wouldn't all of us*, sleep much better tonight if we knew that H. Rap Brown . . . (pause) . . . was somewhere quietly running his *own* little drugstore?"

When the friend who had been present told me that story a few years later, we both laughed. Not at any prescience on Mr. Bundy's part but at a certain dramatic irony: that classic device in which an ignorant speaker occasionally utters unintended truths layered with meanings he neither understands nor suspects. Because, when I heard the story a few years later, not H. Rap Brown but the Imam Al-Amin, peaceably studying his religion and building an Islamic congregation, was indeed the proprietor of a small community grocery store *cum* culture center in Atlanta's West End. . . .

The next episode in this remarkable story might be seen as a tale of two utterly incompatible and mutually exclusive stories. One is the narrative of H. Rap Brown, the armed militant, prone to violence, "revolutionary" or "criminal" depending on your take. This old narrative is preserved alive and well in the computerized memory banks of law enforcement and the film clips and sound bytes of the media, a convenient ghost to be summoned up at will over the next thirty years.

"Y' know," Ed explained. "Something happens. Say the first attempt to bomb the Trade Center, right? They feed their infallible profile into their computer. Muslim . . . radical . . . violent . . . anti-American, whatever, who knows. Anyway, boom, out spits the names, H. Rap Brown prominent among them. Next thing the Feds come storming into the community and haul Jamil in. This actually happened. Of course it's stupid. And every time they have to let him go. But how do you stop it? A goddamn nightmare, they never quit."

Then there is a more contemporary contending narrative, that of the Imam Al-Amin—pious ascetic scholar/teacher and community leader widely perceived to have renounced violence—only to have his hard-won peace plagued at regular intervals by the ghost of the past persona, conjured up to that end.

Or, some suggest, could not the narratives occasionally merge: with the clerical robes and books by the Imam being occasionally discarded for the weapons and fatigues of the militant?

One person had no doubt. "No, Bro. It was just continuous harassment, pure and simple," Ed Brown says. "Harassment, sometimes routine and petty, sometimes pretty serious. Just one damn thing after another. No matter how absurd. The police simply would not leave my brother alone . . . an ongoing police vendetta."

Out of this series of low-level annoyances two incidents stand out. Immediately after the first bombing at the World Trade Center, Imam Al-Amin was arbitrarily hauled in, interrogated, and released under heavy and continuous surveillance, all in the absence of any evidence at all connecting him to the bombing—at least none the authorities cared to disclose.

Another such incident took place in August 1995. A month after a local shooting, agents of the FBI's Domestic Terrorism Task Force and the Bureau of Alcohol, Tobacco and Firearms converged on Atlanta and arrested Imam Al-Amin as the shooter. At a press conference, they informed the press that the victim had identified the Imam as his assailant. The charges were dropped when the victim—who subsequently joined the Imam's mosque—told the press that he had *not* seen his assailant but had been threatened by the authorities with jail if he did not implicate Imam Al-Amin. The whole thing stank of set-up and police impropriety. However, the mainstream civil liberties establishment was silent, so it was left to the national Islamic community to question the irregularities surrounding this incident.

On August 28, 1995, the Washington-based Council on American–Islamic Relations (CAIR), joined by several other national Muslim organizations, called a press conference calling for a Justice Department investigation.

AMERICAN MUSLIM ORGANIZATIONS CALL FOR JUSTICE DEPARTMENT INVESTIGATION OF MUSLIM LEADER'S ARREST

WASHINGTON, D.C. (August 28, 1995) - On Monday, August 8, several national Islamic organizations held a news conference in Washington, DC, to call for a Justice Department investigation into the recent arrest of Imam Jamil Al-Amin. The groups represented at the news conference included the Islamic Society of North America (ISNA), American Muslim Council (AMC), the Muslim Public Affairs Council (MPAC), and the Council on American-Islamic Relations (CAIR). Imam Al-Amin was also in attendance. The joint statement released at the news conference read as follows:

"We the undersigned American Muslim organizations wish to express our deep concern over the recent arrest of Imam Jamil Abdullah Al-Amin, one of the Muslim community's leading figures. The manner of his arrest for aggravated assault and the events that have transpired since the arrest indicate that there is apparently much more to this incident than has been revealed so far. We have several questions about the handling of this case:

1) Why were agents of the FBI, the FBI's Domestic Counterterrorism Task Force and the Bureau of Alcohol, Tobacco and Firearms involved in a case that the police themselves described as a "routine aggravated assault?"

2) Why was the victim in this case, as he himself has stated and The Atlanta Journal reported, threatened with legal charges if he failed to identify Imam Al-Amin as his assailant? And why did authorities refuse to accept the victim's repeated statements that he did not see who the assailant was?

3) Why would the authorities in Atlanta wish to implicate Imam Al-Amin in this case?

4) Why was Imam Al-Amin arrested weeks after the alleged incident, even though he is easily accessible to law enforcement officials at his public place of business? Why was he arrested in his car and not called in for questioning at police facilities?

These and other questions must be answered by those who are in a position of authority over those involved in the inci-

Jamil Abdullah Al-Amin, circa 1997. Photographer unknown; from the collection of Ed Brown.

dent. It is with this goal in mind that we call upon the Justice Department to initiate an immediate investigation into this matter and to report its findings to the American public.

On August 7, Imam Jamil Abdullah Al-Amin, formerly known as H. Rap Brown, was arrested in connection with a July shooting. At the time of the arrest, law enforcement authorities, including the FBI's Joint Counterterrorism Task Force and the Bureau of Alcohol, Tobacco and Firearms (ATF), claimed the shooting victim had identified Imam Al-Amin as the assailant.

The shooting victim, who attended the news conference, now says he does not know who wounded him and that the police pressured him into making the identification. News articles in both The Atlanta Journal and Constitution and The New York Times quote the shooting victim as saying he repeatedly insisted to the police that he did not see who shot him and that it was the police who first presented him with the name and photograph of Imam Al-Amin. The alleged complainant also said he was threatened with legal charges if he did not agree to identify the Imam as the person who shot him.

Imam Al-Amin became a Muslim in the 1970s and has lived in Atlanta for the past 19 years. He is the Imam, or leader, of the Community Mosque in that city. Imam Al-Amin is also recognized as one of several national leaders in the American Muslim community.

Good questions. I am not aware of a response from the Department of Justice. Unfortunately, this is not where the story ends.

Five years later, on Thursday night, March 16, 2000, the troubled relationship between the brother and the various law enforcement agencies would escalate from farce to tragedy. As I write, Imam Al-Amin sits in prison awaiting trial on four felony murder charges for which the state is seeking the death penalty. By the time you read this, the trial will have taken place, so we will have learned the quality and extent of the evidence the state has been able to produce in support of the thirteen charges it has brought. Here is the background— what we know of it at this time.

On the night of March 16, an exchange of gunfire between two Fulton County Sheriff's deputies and persons unknown resulted in the death of Deputy Richard Kinchen and the serious injury of Deputy Aldranon English. The incident took place in the vicinity of the community mosque founded by Imam Al-Amin. According to the authorities, the deputies were attempting to serve an arrest warrant on Al-Amin, who had missed an earlier court appearance. (These charges, while not insignificant, were relatively minor compared to the ones he now faces. Imam Al-Amin maintains that he never received notification of this court date, even though his residence and business address were well known to authorities.)

In the immediate aftermath of the shootings, the Atlanta police released in rapid succession, and the media reported, four significantly different accounts of the incident. The precise location, the sequence of events, the description, and even the number of assailants were all revised in these early accounts, the only constant being a "trail of blood." Deputy English was certain he'd seen, spoken to, shot, and seriously wounded his attacker. The investigators reported following a "heavy trail" of blood up the steps and across the porch of an empty house. From photographs shown him, the wounded officer identified the shooter as Al-Amin, although there were discrepancies in his initial description of the shooter. A regional manhunt was launched. The local media had a field day with H. Rap Brown, whom they identified as a former Black Panther leader and all-around desperado. Apparently the most recent picture they could find was a police mug shot of a fierce-looking Black Power militant out of the 1960s. This image saturated all media (except radio) and is indicative of the general tone of the coverage. However, a few days after the shooting, when Al-Amin was arrested in Alabama, he was found to be completely free of any physical injury. Subsequently very little was heard of the "wounded assailant" and the "trail of blood" motif.

There are other significant discrepancies between police and media reports and the known facts, but there is no need to recapitulate those here. They will come out in court, and I am no more the imam's lawyer than you are a jury of his peers. There is, however, one important dimension to this story that seems to have escaped the notice of the media.

Neither I nor the media commentators, not having been present, can say exactly what happened that night: who was present, or why and how things happened as they did. All that is indisputably clear is that an eminently avoidable human tragedy took place. One young black man was dead, another seriously injured, and a leader of the community was on trial for his life. Was this inevitable? Did any of it have to happen or was it at all avoidable? Recall with me the prevailing context against which these events unfolded.

In March 2000, there was a particular mood in working-class African American communities across the country. Our communities had been traumatized by a series of shootings of unarmed black men in urban centers, most of them innocent of any crime, at the hands of police. In black Islamic communities in particular, feelings were extremely raw over the police shooting of a devout, law-abiding, unarmed young African Muslim named Amadou Diallo as he stood in the foyer of his apartment building in New York. Although over forty shots were fired at or into the young man, the four police perpetrators had been found innocent of any wrongdoing. The Diallo case had been the subject of sermons in mosques across the nation, and the Atlanta mosque was no exception. Let us remember Sura 42, verse 41, "Those who fight when oppressed incur no guilt . . ."

The Atlanta shootout took place within a month of the acquittal of the four cops. One has to wonder, therefore, why, in the climate created by those events, the Atlanta authorities chose to act as they did. Why was it necessary to send into a Muslim community, under cover of darkness, heavily armed men wearing flak jackets to bring in a respected and beloved religious leader, a figure of fixed address and regular and predictable habits, at night? And this in service of a warrant for charges they describe as relatively minor. Who authorized this action and in this manner? Was this abysmally poor judgment or deliberate provocation?

His neighbors also found it passing strange. "He understood the process, how City Hall works, how federal government works," one lady recalls. "So he was like a mayor to many people. Someone people could go to to make things happen." Another pointed out that "Jamil walked up and down the street all day, from the house to the shop to the mosque. So why would they wait 'til ten o'clock at night? The man certainly wasn't hard to find."

There was a conference marking the foundation of the Student Nonviolent Coordinating Committee a few months after the Atlanta shootings. The prisoner's colleagues from the movement said it well in a statement from the conference:

> *While we are deeply saddened by the bloodshed and loss of human life in this tragic and very avoidable incident, we are equally concerned by the presence in the record of a number of factors which threaten to compound tragedy with injustice. We refer to the number of glaring discrepancies in the official version of events and what appears to us as a precipitous and uncritical rush to judgment by the public media.*
>
> *What further distresses us is that the facts as alleged are so completely out of character with the man we have come to know as Imam Jamil Abdullah Al-Amin. For twenty years, our brother has shown himself a serious student of religion, a devout spiritual teacher as well as a public spirited community leader.*
>
> *We ourselves know him as a principled, compassionate, mature black man committed to justice for his people and the moral welfare of his community. These allegations are totally antithetical to the character of a man we greatly respect. We urge therefore a suspension of judgment pending a thorough investigation, not only of the tragic events of March 16, but of the chain of events preceding them. (SNCC 40th Anniversary Conference, Raleigh, N.C., April 16, 2000)*

Imam Al-Amin has been incarcerated since March 2000 under conditions that seem unnecessarily draconian. In solitary confinement, he was for a time deprived of his Holy Qur'an, and he has never been permitted to participate in weekly Jumu'ah services with other members of his faith. He is silenced by a gag order imposed by the court. However, prior to this order he was able to make a personal statement. In the manner of his vocation and faith, the statement is issued in the name of his God, which inclines me to assume its sincerity. We should let him speak in his own voice:

In the name of Allah, the Beneficent the Merciful
Praise be to Allah,
The Cherisher and Sustainer of the Worlds;
Most Gracious, Most Merciful;
Master of the Day of Judgment.
Thee do we worship,
And Thine aid we seek.
Show us the straight way.
Peace be upon those who do good.

My name is Imam Jamil Abdullah Al-Amin, the former H. Rap Brown. I am a devoted servant of Allah, and an unwavering devotee to His cause. For more than 30 years, I have been tormented and persecuted by my enemies for reasons of race and belief. I seek truth over a lie; I seek justice over injustice; I seek righteousness over the rewards of evildoers, and I love Allah more than I love the state.

On March 16, 2000, Fulton County Sheriff Deputy Ricky Kinchen was killed and Sheriff Aldranon English was shot and injured in the neighborhood where I have lived, worked, and prayed. Indeed, this tragedy occurred across the street from the Mosque I founded. I have been accused by the State of Georgia of having committed these crimes. Let me declare before the families of these men, before the state, and any who would dare to know the truth, that I neither shot nor killed anyone. I am innocent of the 13 charges that have been brought against me. Let me also declare that I am one with the grief of this mother and father at the loss of their son. I am joined at the heart with this widow and her children at the loss of a husband and a father. I drink from the same bitter cup of sorrow as the siblings at the loss of a beloved brother. I am powerless to do anything to ease your pain and suffering except pray that Allah comforts you in your hour of need and grants you peace for the remainder of your days.

. . . Fulton County District Attorney, Paul Howard, as a representative of the state, has asked for my death.

. . . They have sought to marginalize my humanity and humiliate my family. They have done their level best to reduce me to a one-dimensional monster. . . . I am no monster. I am a human being created by Allah and am an instrument of his purpose. I am entitled to every right and every consideration as every other human being including fairness, a fair trial and the presumption of innocence.

. . . Let me declare before the families of these men, before the state, and any who would dare to know the truth, that I neither shot nor killed anyone.

It is now for the state and his fellow citizens to speak. In the national mood following the horrific events of September 11, it will be instructive to see what they say.

Ekwueme Michael Thelwell
Moor of Pelham
December 24, 2001
Pelham, Massachusetts

Introduction

Racism systematically verifies itself when the slave can only break free by imitating the master: by contradicting his own reality. *

When a Black man looks at Black people with a Black mind and Black soul, it is immediately apparent that Black people possess certain unique characteristics which not only distinguish them from whites and negroes, but which have greatly contributed to the survival of Blacks. Whites recognize this and have always attempted to eradicate these characteristics or discredit them. In instances where they have succeeded, negroes have been created.

Negroes have always been close allies of whites in trying to eliminate Black resistance to undesirable acculturation. Negroes see poor and uninstitutionalized Blacks as niggers. They find it necessary to prove to whites that they are not niggers, failing to realize that whites see all Black people as niggers, no matter how rich or how poor.

Some Blacks prefer to be called negroes because they like to distinguish themselves from other Blacks. They fear that if they called themselves Blacks, they might antagonize whites. And if they antagonized whites, they would lose

* This quote was taken from an article written by John O'Neal entitled "Motion in the Ocean," in *Black Theater*, Drama Review, Vol. 12, No. 4.

their position as negroes—the white-appointed overseers of Blacks. Thus, negroes have always tried to aid and impress whites by eliminating Blackness. Negroes know that whites prefer institutionalized Blacks, i.e., Blacks who give their allegiance to white cultural, political, social and economic institutions. Non-institutionalized Blacks are difficult to control, because their allegiance is to Blacks and not to white institutions. It is negroes who strain to send their children to white schools so that the nigger in them may be killed and they may thereby become better institutionalized.

Any action or behavior which is not endorsed by whites, negroes consider "acting a nigger." What was "acting a nigger" two years ago is now accepted as "soul." Naturally, this was endorsed by whites before being accepted by negroes. The conversation in negro america has always been, "What are we going to do about them niggers?" never, "What are we going to do about them white folks?" Negroes always said, "Niggers holding us back!" "Niggers ain't shit!" "Don't go around acting a nigger!"

Negroes say:
Nobody but niggers curse and use "poor English."
Nobody but niggers steal.
Nobody but niggers are always loud.
Nobody but niggers listen to the blues.
Nobody but niggers burn and loot.
Nobody but niggers eat watermelon.
I don't call you nigger 'cause you're mine,
I call you nigger 'cause you shine.

While negroes are saying this about poor and uninstitutionalized Blacks, whites say this about all Blacks. The negro, being unable to recognize who is the true enemy, becomes an enemy of Blacks. Negroes prefer "living" to being free.

To be Black in this country is to be a nigger. To be a nigger is to resist both white and negro death. It is to be free in spirit, if not body. It is the spirit of resistance which has prepared Blacks for the ultimate struggle. This word, "nigger," which is taboo in negro and white america, becomes meaningful in the Black community. Among Blacks it is not uncommon to hear the words, "my nigger," (addressed to a brother as an expression of kinship and brotherhood and respect for having resisted), or "He's a bad nigger!," meaning, He'll stand up for himself. He won't let you down. He'll go down with you. When Blacks call *negroes* "niggers," however, it takes on the negativeness of white and negro usage.

Negroes and whites have wished death to all Blacks, to all niggers. Their sentiment is "Die Nigger Die!"—either by becoming a negro or by institutionalized or active genocide.

Blacks know, however, that no matter how much or how hard negroes and whites may try, ultimately it will be the negro and his allies who will "Dye, die, die!"

> America calling.
> negroes.
> can you dance?
> play foot/baseball?
> nanny?
> cook?
> needed now. negroes
> who can entertain
> ONLY.
> others not
> wanted.
> (& are considered extremely dangerous.)
>
> Don L. Lee

1 My first contact with white america was marked by her violence, for when a white doctor pulled me from between my mother's legs and slapped my wet ass, I, as every other negro in america, reacted to this man-inflicted pain with a cry. A cry that america has never allowed to cease; a cry that gets louder and more intense with age; a cry that can only be heard and understood by others who live behind the color curtain. A cry? Or was it a scream? Whatever it was, we accepted it.

I had been born in "america, the land of the free." To insure my country's freedom, my father was somewhere fighting, for this was a year of the second war to end all wars—World War II. This was October 4, 1943, and victory was in the air. The world would now be safe for democracy.

But who would insure my freedom? Who would make democracy safe for Black people? America recognized long ago what negroes now examine in disbelief: every Black birth in america is political. With each new birth comes a potential challenge to the existing order. Each new generation brings forth untested militancy. America's ruling class now experiences what Herod must have at the birth of "Christ": "Go and search . . . and when ye have found him, bring me word again, that I may come and worship him also." America doesn't know which Black birth is going to be the birth that will overthrow this country.

The threat to america, however, does not exist in negro america, but rather as a result of negro america. If one examines the structure of this country closely he will note that there are three basic categories: they are white america, negro america, and Black america. The threat to the existing structure comes from Black america, which exists in contradiction to both white and negro america. It is the evolution of these contradictions that has given rise to the present revolutionary conditions. Revolution is indeed inevitable, and, as the cycle of change closes around america's racist environment, the issue of color becomes more pertinent.

Color is the first thing Black people in america become aware of. You are born into a world that has given color meaning and color becomes the single most determining factor of your existence. Color determines where you live, how you live and, under certain circumstances, if you will live. Color determines your friends, your education, your mother's and father's jobs, where you play, what you play and, more importantly, what you think of yourself.

In and of itself, color has no meaning. But the white world has given it meaning—political, social, economic, historical, physiological and philosophical. Once color has been given meaning, an order is thereby established. If you are born Black in america, you are the last of that order. As kids we learned the formula for the structure of american society:

If you're white,
You're all right.
If you're brown,
Stick around.
But if you're black,
Get back, get back.

Because of the importance assigned to color, negroes choose only to legitimatize two americas: white and negro. When one examines the way in which these two americas are structured, it is obvious that the similarities between them are greater than the differences. The differences exist only in the

2

external control of each and their internal order, which, in turn, create value contradictions. In other words, whites control both white america and negro america for the benefit of whites. And because of this kind of external control by whites in their own self-interest, negroes who structure their communities after those of whites are forced to enforce values of whites. They attempt to explain away their lack of control by saying that they are just members of the larger community of "americans."

A monologue is perpetually expounded by white america which is echoed by negroes afflicted with white patriotism.

white america:
Think white or I'll kill you.
And if you think too white, I'll kill you.
negro america:
Think white or I'll kill you.
And if you think too white "the man" will kill you.
So think colored.
Imitate the white man,
but not to perfection in front of him.

As Julian Moreau says in his novel, *Black Commandos*:

Attitudes necessary for survival were vigorously pounded into the wooly heads of black boys and girls by their loving mothers. The boys were reared to be Negroes, not men. A Negro might survive a while, but a black "man" didn't live very long. . . . A black boy aiming to reach "manhood" rather than "Negro-hood" rarely lived that long.

For 400 years the internal contradictions and inconsistencies of white america have been dealt with through its institutions. In regard to race or color, these contradictions have

3

always been on a national, never a local or individual level. Whites as individuals have always loved to be thought of as superior. They have always known that if they could justify and make their actions legal, either through their religion, their courts or their history (educational system), then it would be unnecessary to actually rectify them because the negro would accept their interpretation. White america's most difficult problem thus becomes how to justify and not rectify national inconsistencies. If white nationalism is disguised as history or religion, then it is irrefutable. White nationalism divides history into two parts, B.C. and A.D.— before the white man's religion and after it. And "progress," of course, is considered to have taken place only after the white man's religion came into being. The implication is evident: God is on the white man's side, for white Jesus was the "son" of God.

White america has used religion and history to its advantage. Thus, the North never really differed from the South for they both taught the same history. Catholics never differed from other religions for they taught from the same text. Republicans are no different from Democrats, as Democrats are no different from Dixiecrats. As for liberals, Fanon says they are "as much the enemy of oppressed people and Freedom as the self-avowed enemy, because it is impossible to be both a member of the oppressor class and a friend of the oppressed." So we can see that for white america the only real contradictions are those that arise from the Thirteenth, Fourteenth and Fifteenth Amendments of her Constitution. These contradictions give rise to negro america.

Most Black persons of my time were born into negro america. The first thing you learn is that you are different from whites. The next thing you learn is that you are different from each other. You are born into a world of double standards where color is of paramount importance. In your

4

cer things happen with **ghter, clearer skin!**

nicer things happen wit **brighter, clearer ski**

Mirror, mir
on the wall
what's the
prettiest
wig of all?

Considering the amazi
low prices, why not order a whole wardrobe of hair-piece
Wouldn't that be exciting?

Enjoy the
LIGHT
Side of Life...

*"A Whole
New
World
has opened
up to me"*

community a color pattern exists which is closely akin to the white man's, and likewise reinforced from both ends of the spectrum. Light-skinned negroes believe they are superior and darker negroes allow them to operate on that belief. Because of the wide color range which exists in negro america, an internal color colony has been created. Dark negroes are taught that they are inferior not only to whites but to lighter-skinned negroes. And lighter-skinned negroes assume a superior attitude.

Negro america is set up the same as white america. The lighter skinned a negro, the more significant a role he can play. (It has always been the one who looked white who made it in negro america. This was the man with the position, the influence, this was the man who usually got the white man's best job.) In between light negro america and Black negro america (in terms of color), there is a special category of people, who are assigned the name of red niggers. These are the people who are light enough to go into light negro america, but do not have caucasian characteristics. They don't have straight hair or white features. So they can go either way, depending on them. They can operate in Black negro america or at the outer fringes of light negro america. Race prejudice in america becomes color prejudice in negro america. That which is cultural prejudice by whites against Blacks becomes class prejudice in negro america. To distinguish themselves, negroes assign class distinctions. Here we find the instituting and substituting of parallel values. Negroes assume that what is good for white america is good for negro america.

Negroes are always confined to what can be called the "shit regiment." I first became acquainted with the shit regiment in the cub scouts. In every parade, we always marched behind the horses, which meant that we always had to march in horseshit. All the way through life there are shit regiments in the negro community and negroes adhere to them. As a matter of fact, negroes will protect these regiments. The debate was never whether or not we had to march, but whether or not the whites were going to put machines down there to wash the horseshit away before we marched in it. There was never any discussion as to whether or not we should march behind the horses. Uh-uh. Everybody accepted that. They just wanted the horseshit washed out of the way before we came through. White america's largest shit regiment is negro america.

Given that negroes are a colonized people, the most important phase of colonization is the sub-cultural phase. In negro america, negroes relate only to negroes of the same educational background. Dr. So-and-So talks only to Dr. So-and-So and the brother on the block better not act like he thinks he can go up to Dr. So-and-So and talk to him man-to-man. To Dr. So-and-So, the brother on the block is nothing but a nigger who's holding the race back. Dr. So-and-So goes to the Episcopal Church, the Presbyterian or the Catholic Church. The brother on the block goes to the Baptist Church, the Holy Rollers or the Sanctified Church. And the Methodist Church is in between the two. It ain't as niggerish as the Baptist Church, but it's not as high class as the Episcopal Church. As negroes become more "white-educated," the transition in religion begins. All of a sudden, it's beneath them to go to church and shout and get happy. That's not dignified. As they get more "educated," their religion gets more like the white man's religion as if their heaven will be segregated too. "Education" even extends down to the naming of the children. The more "educated" the negro becomes, the more European names he picks for his children. Michele, Simone, Hubert, Whitney. All of a sudden, Sam and Bertha Lee ain't good enough anymore. In other words, values are

8

assigned to names. Names must now be more than functional.

The poor negro doesn't aspire to be white, he just wants to make it into negro america. So he works hard all his life and finally rents a little house and puts some furniture in it which he keeps covered with plastic so it won't get dirty. And he gets mad if anybody sits on it, because he's trying to imitate negro america. Once he gets into negro america, he learns of so-called middle-class values, white values. Then he wants to get into white america.

When he tries to enter white america, he is rejected. The doors are shut. Even if he has a big job in some white firm, if he's one of those "only" negroes, he still finds out that he's Black when it's quitting time. The white workers go their way and leave him to go his. They're nice and friendly on the job and all buddy-buddy, but that doesn't go outside the office. They don't want their friends thinking that they're nigger lovers. So this sets up a reaction in the negro. He gets frustrated and tries to live a contradiction and that's why when the rebellions start, he's all for them. He doesn't have the courage to admit it to the white man. When the white folks he works with ask him what he thinks about "the riot," he says it's hurting the cause and all sorts of bull like that. But that night after work, he breaks records getting home to watch it on t.v., cheering like a muthafucka the whole time. Take the Washington, D.C., rebellion, for instance. They arrested something like 3,000 people and when they booked 'em, they found out that the great majority of them worked for the government. Had jobs, making money, still these were the dudes who were out in the street. In Detroit it was the same thing. It wasn't only the unemployed brother. It was the one who was bringing home $110 every Friday. It was the one who had a Thunderbird, and some clean vines. He was the one who had tried to enter white america and had found that no matter what he did, he was still a nigger to the white man.

Those Black people who remain in the Black community, however, remain a viable force. They don't have the frustrations that exist in negro america. In Black america the bonds are tighter. The fight is for freedom, not whiteness.

Negroes have always been treated like wild, caged animals by the white man, and have always felt the passions of caged animals (because they were living in cages), but they would always act civilized with whites, that is, what white people told them was civilized. But inside this "civilized" negro was an undying hate. This hate, however, could only be released in negro america. If it was ever released in white america, it would prove to white people that negroes were savages. That hate became a self-hate. So to preserve their sanity, their humanity and their white civilization, negroes had to hate themselves. And when they hated, they distinguished between those who were most like white people and those who were Black. And they hated Black people and poor negroes. (Poor negroes are those Black people with the values of negro america, but not the means.)

It is clear that the revolution will not come from negro america but from Black america, and Black america is growing. Black america is important because it is here that you will find the self-imposed exiles from both white and negro america. Black america has always offered Blacks human freedoms—a humanism uncommon to white and negro america. Some enter Black america because negro america rejects darker-skinned negroes, and, of course, if a person is rejected by negro america, he is automatically rejected by white america. Other people enter Black america because of some experience they had in their childhood. Still others, because of something they may have read that was written by some-

10

one in Black america. Black america has existed ever since the first slave despised the injustice that was done to him and did not seek to accommodate himself to that injustice. Thus, there have always been people who could articulate these injustices and could discuss what the response to these injustices should be. It is self-evident that people always rebel against oppression and there has been one continuous rebellion in Black america since the first slave got here.

2 I was born into a family of dark-skinned negroes, but I'm what many consider a red nigger. My mother, my father, my brother Ed and my sister are all darker than I am. Because I was lighter, it meant that I was supposed to get ahead. So my mother gave me what I would call preferential treatment. Because of this there was a lot of rivalry between my brother Ed and myself. He and I weren't "tight" when we were young. He thought that our mother treated me better than she did him. In negro america the more you look like buttermilk, the prettier you're supposed to be. This is color prejudice. I don't think that my mother was conscious of all this, but it happened a lot of times. So Ed and I used to have a lot of conflicts. I didn't want it that way. Ed was my older brother and I looked up to him. But he didn't want me hanging around him.

Ed and I are very close now and that color thing doesn't come between us anymore. But it's a thing which could really damage the Black community if people don't begin to understand it. There are nationalist groups that won't accept light-complexioned Blacks. What they're doing is helping the white man, because they're creating the potential for a divisive fight inside the Black community. And it's totally unnecessary and damaging. The government is doing enough to try and divide the Black community. We shouldn't be helping them. We must learn that Black is not a color but the way you think.

If we are to succeed in the struggle we must eliminate the significance that we have assigned to color in our community. The range of Black runs from the brother who is Black enough to poot smoke, to the blood who is pale with the rape of Mothers. Among Black people color can have no value, no significance. Commitment will determine the value of individuals. If I had identified with the attitudes of white-minded negroes and then come home to my dark-skinned brother and family, I wouldn't have been able to accept them. But that wasn't a problem for me, because I knew who I wanted to identify with. It was the bloods in my neighborhood, the guys who hung out down on the corner. The Black community, in other words. I always hung out with cats who had made hanging out a profession. I found that it took special skills to hang out 14 hours just laying and playing.

My first institutionalized schooling came in an orphanage —Blundon Orphanage Home. It was operated by white missionaries whose role was similar to that of whites in Africa. Civilize the savage through Christianity. Savages in this case being Black kids from families too poor to support them. The school had the look of a huge plantation with two big shabby old buildings located near the bottom of the hill and a relatively well-kept building at the top. The grounds around the building at the top of the hill were also well-kept with trees and shrubs and Keep-Off signs. More attention, in fact, was paid to the grounds on the "hill" than was paid to the two buildings in the "Bottom." Each of the "Big Houses," as they were called, had classrooms on the bottom floors and living quarters above. All of the teachers and students in the school were Black. The Black residents were of all ages and basically responsible for each other. The older children attended to the needs of the smaller children. Children of all ages were expected to work and were assigned jobs.

This was my first real contact with a world bigger and badder than that of my street. You had to excel in either fighting, running or tomming; I integrated the three. In this world, the heroes were bloods who will never be remembered outside our Black community. Cats like Pie-man, Ig, Yank, Smokey, Hawk, Lil Nel—all bad muthafuckas. Young bloods wanted to be like these brothers. They were the men in our community. They had all the women and had made their way to the top through sports and knowing the streets. So to us, the most important thing was to excel in athletics. Recess was the most essential part of the school day, for we could practice our skills. One play could make or break you. We all lived for the big play. For many it never came.

Once I'd established my reputation, cats respected it. "You don't mess with Rap, cause he's our man." If I went out of my neighborhood, though, it was another story. I'd be on somebody else's turf and would have to make it or take it over there. So there was always a lot of fighting and competition among the young brothers.

It really gets bad when you get to high school. In high school there's always rivalry between the football teams of the two high schools in town or something like that. But it's more than athletic rivalry. It may start on the football field, but it's carried to the street. In Baton Rouge there was a rivalry between McKinley High and Capitol High. You'd think the students were two totally different races. People were perpetually at war. I mean they were really at war. Gangs from South Baton Rouge would be expected to fight dudes from the Park. Dudes from the Park couldn't come to South Baton Rouge and vice-versa unless they were *bad* muthafuckas. And if they were caught, being bad didn't make no difference.

That type of rivalry still exists. It's perpetuated by the schools, by the negroes in authority who pretend they're handling it, but don't. The whole fever pitch which builds up in those gangs is transferred from the people who are being "educated" to the cats who hang around the streets.

15

But when most of us rivals went on to college, then college made a kind of bond between us. The athletes who had scholarships and the cats who worked during the summer to get that tuition came to college and then they became allies against dudes from other cities. Like, "you my homeboy, and the dude who ain't from around here, he ain't one of us." Yeah, well that's part of that whole primitive thing and it's very dangerous. Given the destruction by slavery of both tribe and culture, negroes created a new kind of american tribalism. A tribalism based on the exclusion of certain types. A deliberate attempt to make race a secondary consideration. There are tribes and tribes of negroes. The A.K.A. tribe, Kappa tribe, Doctor tribe, Teacher tribe, Entertainer tribe, High School tribe, College tribe, etc. This tribalism has extended into what is called the "Movement." "Militant" tribes compete against other "militant" tribes and "moderate" tribes, to promote tribal interests and not the interests of the race or the masses. We treat revolution as if it is an historic process rather than an evolutionary movement. In other words, we all got a monopoly on truth. Whites who consider themselves allies add to this by deciding which tribe is "correct" and which is "incorrect." In other words, the one which best fits their needs. As a result of this kind of external control, tribes engage in fratricide (unknowingly in most cases) to gain the favor of the white "ally." Tribe is placed above race. It is not uncommon to hear negroes say, "My loyalty is to my Frat., God, and my country, in that order."

When a race of people is oppressed within a system that fosters the idea of competitive individualism, the political polarization around individual interests prevents group interests. Each negro prides himself on his ability to reason or think as an individual. Therefore, any gains are to the individual and not to the group. So individuals join tribes or groups to further their own personal ambitions. It's one of

16

the things that keeps us fighting ourselves instead of the enemy. Black people have always been ready to shoot and cut each other up. The weekend is always wartime in the Black community. Every week when Friday rolls around, you know that somebody is gon' get killed before church time Sunday morning. But let one white man come down the street acting bad and all he got in his pocket is a toothpick, all of them bad niggers, niggers ready to kill in a minute, be hiding in the alleys or be grinning and bowing. "Yassuh, Mr. White Man." White bleeds just as red as Black does, but you can only prove it by hearsay. And the press has done a job on negroes and whites, because it makes you think that Black people are killing 14 white folks a day. But even J. Edgar Hoover, with his faggot ass, admits that more Black folks kill Black folks than Blacks kill whites. But everybody thinks that we're killing white folks. Uh-uh. We're still killing off each other. Even a lot of these so-called "militants" go around pulling their 22's on Black people and "tomming" when the white man comes around. And they supposed to be so muthafucking bad. Yeah, we are bad when it comes to us. And the white man sits back and laughs 'cause niggers ain't got no better sense than to be fighting one another.

However, we must understand the many ways in which the white man brainwashes people into acting and thinking like he wants them to so he can continue to control them.

You grow up in Black america and it's like living in a pressure cooker. Babies become men without going through childhood. And when you become a man, you got nothing to look forward to and nothing to look back on. So what do you make it on? The wine bottle, the reefer or Jesus. A taste of grape, the weed or the cross. These are our painkillers.

I knew dudes who were old men by the time they were seven. That's the age when little white kids are dreaming about fairy princesses and Cinderella and playing in tree houses and wondering whether they want two cars or four cars when they grow up. We didn't have time for all that. Didn't even have time for childhood. If you acted like a child, you didn't survive and that's all there was to it. Hell, you be walking home from school and up come some high school dudes who'd jack you up and take the little dime your mama had given you to buy some candy with. So what'd you do? Jump some dude who was younger and littler than you and take his dime. And pretty soon you started carrying a razor blade, a switch blade or just a pocketful of rocks so you could protect yourself as a man. You had to if you were going to survive.

White folks get all righteous and wonder why Black people steal and gamble. Same reason white folks do. We need money, because the society says you must have it to keep from starving. If you got it, you eat. If you don't, tough. But white people are able to make their stealing and gambling legitimate. White man'll sell you a $20 suit for $50 and call it good business. What he actually did was steal $30. White man'll buy a watch for $5.00 sell it for $49.95 and call the difference, profit. Profit is a nice word for stealing which the society has legitimatized. Catholics go to church every week and gamble, but they call it Bingo. The Pope blesses 'em, so it's all right. The state of Nevada is built on a deck of cards and a roulette wheel, but that's okay, 'cause it's white folks that passed the law saying it was okay. But you let us get over in the corner of the alley with some dice and try to make a little profit and here come the police, the judge, the jailer and the sociology student. We get thrown into jail for gambling or stealing. White folks go to Congress for stealing and they call that democracy.

America is a country that makes you want things, but doesn't give you the means to get those things. Little Black children sit in front of the t.v. set and all they see are fine cars, perfumes, clothes and everything else they ain't got. They sit there and watch it, telling the rats to sit down and stop blocking their view. Ain't nobody told them, though, that they don't have any way of getting any of that stuff. They couldn't even get full at supper, but that don't matter. They want an Oldsmobile. So next day during recess, they go off in a corner of the schoolyard and pitch pennies, play Odd Man Wins, Heads-up Basketball for a quarter, Pitty-Pat for a nickel, Old Maid for a penny. Once they become pros at that, they move on up to Tonk, Black Jack and Craps. After school, there's the pinball machines. Some of them little dudes could barely see the game board, but they would be there, jim, shoving nickels in the machine, trying to manipulate the lights into a straight line. You could win 50 cents or a dollar and if you were lucky, $5.00. Once you graduated from the pinball machine, you entered the poolroom.

America's a bitch. Being Black in this country is like somebody asking you to play white Russian roulette and giving you a gun with bullets in all the chambers. Any way you go, jim, that's your ass. America says you got to have money to live and to get money you got to have a job. To get a job, you got to have an education. So along comes a Black man and he gets a worse than inferior education so he can't qualify for a job he couldn't get because he was Black to begin with and still he's supposed to eat, keep his family together, pay the rent and buy an Oldsmobile. And white folks wonder why niggers steel and gamble. I only wish we would stop this petty stealing and take care of Chase Manhattan Bank, Fort Knox or some armories.

There was this blood I grew up with named J.S. He was a smart dude, particularly in math. Dude would have given a computer competition. He lived with his aunt, who worked as a maid, and three sisters. Cause his aunt was a maid, she didn't make hardly nothing. White folks love to pay their niggers in old clothes and leftovers. So he couldn't dress like some of the other students whose parents were making it in negro america. The teachers were all trying to make it in negro america too. They took a bath once a day and wiped under their arms and between their legs twice a day and always tried to smell like they lived in perfume bottles. Well, I know how my man must've felt sitting in class in front of some bitch like this. He felt like a piece of shit, particularly when the teacher would stand up in front of the class and talk about him 'cause his clothes were dirty. You damned right his clothes were dirty! His aunt worked from can to can't, and by the time she got home at night she was too tired to bend over the scrub board to wash out some clothes for J.S. to wear every day. She did the best she could.

J.S. was as smart as anybody in school and he showed it, too, but in negro america if you didn't have the right color, the right clothes, and the right manners, sorry for you. Them teachers were slick, though, when it came to telling a kid he wasn't shit. They were always going out of the room to stand in the hall and gossip with the other teachers. When they did, they'd leave a student in charge to sit behind the desk and take the names of the students who talked or cut up. And always, the one left in charge was light, bright and almost white. If a light-skinned student was reciting in class, the teacher had the patience of Job, the understanding of Solomon and the expectations of God Almighty himself. But you let a sho-nuf blood just pause when he was reciting and the teacher told him to sit down in a voice filled with hatred. "I didn't expect you to know it anyway," the teacher would sometimes say, meaning, you're black. You're black! You're black!

The teachers had to tell J.S. he was smart, 'cause it was so obvious. But they made a point of letting him know that being smart wasn't enough if your hair was uncombed, your clothes a little dirty, your skin a little ashy and your manners not the best. In other words, you may be smart, but you black! So J.S. learned pretty quick that there wasn't no reward in being smart and that it didn't have a damned thing to do with surviving.

But this is the kind of education we were subjected to. Education ain't just what comes out of the books, but it's everything that goes on in the school. And if you leave school hating yourself, then it doesn't matter how much you know. Education in america has to be viewed as propaganda machinery. All educational systems are propaganda machines, but for Black people, the american educational system is a propaganda machine we don't need. It propagandizes against us. It makes us hate ourselves.

I began realizing this when I was in high school. I saw no sense in reading Shakespeare. After I read Othello, it was obvious that Shakespeare was a racist. From reading his poetry, I gathered that he was a faggot. But we never discussed the racist attitude expressed in his works. This was when I really began to raise questions. I was in constant conflict with my teachers in high school. I would interpret the thing one way and they would say it's wrong. Well, how could they tell me what Shakespeare was thinking. I knew then that something was wrong, unless the teachers had a monopoly on truth or were communicating with the dead.

Part of my mother's whole attempt to make us a part of negro america was that she took us out of McKinley High and sent us to Southern High. Anybody who could pay $12 a year could go and that was for the activities card. So, you see how jive the thing was. It was connected with the negro college in Baton Rouge, Southern University, and it was really set up so the teachers at Southern wouldn't have to send their children to school with Black kids. It was a

21

crock of shit, but it had an air of "respectability." This was where all the bourgeois negroes were supposed to go.

It could've created problems for me, because if I had identified with most of the white-minded negroes at school, I wouldn't have been able to relate to brothers on the block. Worse than that, I would've thought that I was better than them. It's like the whole school busing thing now. Busing Black children to schools outside the Black community is nothing but a move to divide the community. If integration is what's wanted, then bus the whole community. But to take individuals out of the community is a very dangerous and immoral thing. The "brightest" students are taken, students who can fit into the white man's program best, and they're bused out of the community so they can come back and articulate the white man's program. That splits the community. Parents who sent their children to white schools in the South made a mistake. They injured those students mentally for life. To send a Black kid to a school full of howling maniacs. Madmen! Wildmen! Animals! And those Black kids got their minds messed up. You send a student to a white school and he has to come home to a Black family and a Black community. It messes him up and it messes the community up. This is a deliberate part of "the man's" game.

I could've gotten messed up like that at Southern High if I hadn't known where it was at and what was happening. But I didn't change myself to fit that phony-ass atmosphere and try to be respectable and all that shit. Me and Southern High had quite a few conflicts. One time I got put out of school for wearing my shirt out of my pants. Another time I got put out for cursing out a teacher.

Ed and my sister, who're both older than I, went to the same school. So when I came along, I had to go through the same teachers they'd gone through. The teachers said I should be just like them. I should open doors for them and shit like that. Just like my family had always said I should do things like Ed. So when I wóuldn't do all these things and started raising hell, my homeroom teacher started criticizing me. One day I got sick of that shit and I cussed her out. I got put out of school for that.

I was always at odds with teachers. There are certain things in negro institutions that you have to do if you expect to make good grades and certain things you don't do. One of those things is you don't talk back. You don't challenge the existing order. Well, I challenge anything that doesn't make good sense.

Another time in high school they called my mother in about me because I got into it with one of the dudes teaching shop. I knew he was screwing my homeroom teacher, so I didn't have no respect for him, especially since I knew his wife. Us young dudes in the Black community directed our aggression against negroes who had these positions because there was a failure on their part to take out their aggression against white people. But, these negroes in position would always direct their grievances toward Black students. They got mad at us 'cause the white man was mistreating them, and we got mad at them 'cause they let the white man mistreat 'em and then turned around and mistreated us, on top of the white man mistreating all of us.

But I stayed in school, 'cause I wasn't willing to get caught in another trick that eventually led to long sentences in jail or ending up in the gutter one night with a knife in your back. A lot of bloods, though, couldn't cut school. When they came, it was to practice the education they'd been getting out in the street. While we were still in elementary school, J.S. would wait for recess to get out to the playground where he'd sneak a deck of cards out of his pocket, get way off in a corner and start gambling. After school, we'd go home and J.S. would go on down to the pool hall. By the time he was fourteen, he was dealing in a gambling club in West Baton Rouge. After a while he quit school. Working at the club like he was, he was ready to go to bed when the rest of us were getting up to go to classes. We used to see him in the afternoon, though. He'd drop by the school and be vined down. He was clean, jim. Had him a conk then and he knew he was ready.

After a while the state police started cracking down on gambling and J.S. cut out of Baton Rouge and started following the action from Biloxi, Mississippi, over to Houston, Texas, and back again. He was sixteen.

It was a couple of years later when I saw him again. I'd just entered college. I was thumbing my way to school when who should I see hanging out on the corner but J.S., looking clean. I went up to him. We greeted each other like we were ol' cut-buddies, but after all the greeting and slapping hands, we found it hard to talk to each other. Too many different kinds of experience had come between us. He was my nigger, but J.S. had made a way of life on the block which I just figured had aged him. It was a rough life. Drinking, fighting, dodging the police, gambling—it can wear a man.down fast. I looked at J.S. and it was beginning to show on him. His eyes once used to shine, but they'd gotten dull and red. His face was getting tight and there were wrinkles starting to crawl across his forehead. He told me that he'd just gotten out of the joint on a concealed weapons charge. Plus he told me that when gambling and living off women wasn't enough to survive, he'd become a cat burglar and a fence on the side. But he definitely wasn't feeling sorry for himself. Only thing he was unhappy about was that his luck in gambling was off. We went and got some "pluck" (wine) and I told him I was in college. He asked what I wanted to be. I told him rich. He looked up at the ceiling and paused for a minute before he said, "You know, I've never given any thought to what I want

24

to become." I told him he should think about it, but I knew I was shuckin' and jivin'. Hell, hardly any of us had ever thought about what we wanted to become. What was the future? That was something white folks had. We just lived from day to day, expecting whatever life put on us and dealing with it the best way we knew how when it came. I had accepted the big lie of a Black man succeeding.

I remembered that J.S. was always good with math. I knew how to count money and always figured I didn't need to know no more about numbers, but I had to take math in college. So I showed J.S. some of the math problems I had been having trouble with and he looked 'em over for a short while and knocked 'em out in no time. He said he'd tutor me in math. I told him that was cool. But that was the last time I saw him. A couple of weeks later he shot and killed some dude and the judge gave him life. He was eighteen.

That's the way the deal goes down for a lot of bloods. Wiped out by the time they're eighteen and don't ever really know why. He was rebelling against the way the cards were stacked against him and even his rebellion was a stacked deck. He lived his life the way he saw it, made his own laws, but what was legal in our world wasn't "legal" in the white world and eventually he went down.

My ol' lady wanted to keep all that away from me. Didn't want me to know anything about it. I guess she called it protecting me, but I had to be out there where the action was. She thought I should be in the house reading books like Ed so I could make my way in negro america, but I wasn't hearing that. I never was one for too much reading anyway. Too, how was I supposed to stay on top of what was going down if I was sitting up in the house with a book. If you were going to stay in control, you had to be in the street.

The street is where young bloods get their education. I learned how to talk in the street, not from reading about

Dick and Jane going to the zoo and all that simple shit. The teacher would test our vocabulary each week, but we knew the vocabulary we needed. They'd give us arithmetic to exercise our minds. Hell, we exercised our minds by playing the Dozens.

I fucked your mama
Till she went blind.
Her breath smells bad,
But she sure can grind.

I fucked your mama
For a solid hour.
Baby came out
Screaming, Black Power.

Elephant and the Baboon
Learning to screw.
Baby came out looking
Like Spiro Agnew.

And the teacher expected me to sit up in class and study poetry after I could run down shit like that. If anybody needed to study poetry, she needed to study mine. We played the Dozens for recreation, like white folks play Scrabble.

In many ways, though, the Dozens is a mean game because what you try to do is totally destroy somebody else with words. It's that whole competition thing again, fighting each other. There'd be sometimes 40 or 50 dudes standing around and the winner was determined by the way they responded to what was said. If you fell all over each other laughing, then you knew you'd scored. It was a bad scene for the dude that was getting humiliated. I seldom was.

That's why they call me Rap, 'cause I could rap. (The name stuck because Ed would always say, "That my nigger Rap," "Rap my nigger.") But for dudes who couldn't, it was like they were humiliated because they were born Black and then they turned around and got humiliated by their own people, which was really all they had left. But that's the way it is. Those that feel most humiliated humiliate others. The real aim of the Dozens was to get a dude so mad that he'd cry or get mad enough to fight. You'd say shit like, "Man, tell your mama to stop coming around my house all the time. I'm tired of fucking her and I think you should know that it ain't no accident you look like me." And it could go on for hours sometimes. Some of the best Dozens players were girls.

Signifying is more humane. Instead of coming down on somebody's mother, you come down on them. But, before you can signify you got to be able to rap. A session would start maybe by a brother saying, "Man, before you mess with me you'd rather run rabbits, eat shit and bark at the moon." Then, if he was talking to me, I'd tell him:

Man, you must don't know who I am.
I'm sweet peeter jeeter the womb beater
The baby maker the cradle shaker
The deerslayer the buckbinder the women finder
Known from the Gold Coast to the rocky shores of Maine
Rap is my name and love is my game.
I'm the bed tucker the cock plucker the motherfucker
The milkshaker the record breaker the population maker
The gun-slinger the baby bringer
The hum-dinger the pussy ringer
The man with the terrible middle finger.
The hard hitter the bullshitter the poly-nussy getter
The beast from the East the Judge the sludge

The women's pet the men's fret and the punks'
  pin-up boy.
They call me Rap the dicker the ass kicker
The cherry picker the city slicker the titty licker
And I ain't giving up nothing but bubble gum and
  hard times and I'm fresh out of bubble gum.
I'm giving up wooden nickels 'cause I know they
  won't spend
And I got a pocketful of splinter change.
I'm a member of the bathtub club: I'm seeing a
  whole lot of ass but I ain't taking no shit.
I'm the man who walked the water and tied the
  whale's tail in a knot
Taught the little fishes how to swim
Crossed the burning sands and shook the devil's
  hand
Rode round the world on the back of a snail
  carrying a sack saying AIR MAIL.
Walked 49 miles of barbwire and used a Cobra
  snake for a necktie
And got a brand new house on the roadside
  made from a cracker's hide,
Got a brand new chimney setting on top made
  from the cracker's skull
Took a hammer and nail and built the world and
  calls it "THE BUCKET OF BLOOD."
Yes, I'm hemp the demp the women's pimp
Women fight for my delight.
I'm a bad motherfucker. Rap the rip-saw the
  devil's brother 'n law.
I roam the world I'm known to wander and this .45
  is where I get my thunder.
I'm the only man in the world who knows why white
  milk makes yellow butter.

I know where the lights go when you cut the switch
   off.
I might not be the best in the world, but I'm in
   the top two and my brother's getting old.

And ain't nothing bad 'bout you but your breath.

Now, if the brother couldn't come back behind that, I
usually cut him some slack (depending on time, place and
his attitude). We learned what the white folks call verbal
skills. We learned how to throw them words together.
America, however, has Black folk in a serious game of the
Dozens. (The dirty muthafucka.) Signifying allowed you a
choice—you could either make a cat feel good or bad. If
you had just destroyed someone or if they were just down
already, signifying could help them over. Signifying was
also a way of expressing your own feelings:

Man, I can't win for losing.
If it wasn't for bad luck, I wouldn't
   have no luck at all.
I been having buzzard luck
Can't kill nothing and won't nothing die
I'm living on the welfare and things is
   stormy
They borrowing their shit from the Salvation
   Army
But things bound to get better 'cause they can't
   get no worse
I'm just like the blind man, standing by a
   broken window
I don't feel no pain.
But it's your world
You the man I pay rent to
If I had your hands I'd give 'way both my arms.

Cause I could do without them
I'm the man but you the main man
I read the books you write
You set the pace in the race I run
Why, you always in good form
You got more foam than Alka Seltzer. . .

Signifying at its best can be heard when brothers are exchanging tales. I used to hang out in the bars just to hear the old men "talking shit." By the time I was nine, I could talk Shine and the Titanic, Signifying Monkey, three different ways, and Piss-Pot-Peet, for two hours without stopping.

Sometimes I wonder why I even bothered to go to school. Practically everything I know I learned on the corner. Today they're talking about teaching sex in school. But that's white folks for you. They got to be taught to screw. They got to intellectualize everything. Now how you gon' intellectualize screwing? At the age when little white kids were finding out that there was something down there to play with, we knew where it went and what to do with it after it got there. You weren't a man if you hadn't gotten yourself a little piece by the time you were seven. When the white kids were out playing Hide and Go Seek, we were playing Hide and Go Get It. One dude would count to a hundred while the girls hid. Once the girls were hidden, you went and found one and you got it. That was the game. Hide and Go Get It. None of that ol' simple tagging a tree and yelling, "I got in free." Yeah, we got in free.

Some of the dudes started pimping early for their sisters and, sometimes, even their mama. Survival'll make you do anything, jim. Anything! You'd be walking down the street one night and some white dude in a car would pull up next to you and say, "Hey, boy, you got a sister?" or, "You know any nice colored girls?" So whitey would get him a little taste of black gold for $10 or $15 and Black people helped him. It shows you just how low you can get when you sell your own women to a white man—or any man for that matter. But it's particularly bad when they're sold to white men. To this day, you can find the snakes in the Black community on the weekends trying to buy some Black pussy. And Black men see 'em, know what they're there for and don't run 'em out. Not even the so-called big, bad militants.

So much of the life story of any negro growing up in america is the story of what has been done to him and how he reacts to that. That's it. White man acts. Negroes react.

My father is a good example of that. He is a laborer. He works for Esso Standard Oil! Mr. Jesse James Rockefeller! When I was young, it often seemed to me that my father appeared to be pissed off. Now I can understand why. He wouldn't take his frustration out on the people he'd like to. So he would take it out on other people. I remember we were one of the first families in the community to get a t.v. First in the sense that all the kids could come and watch it. Other people had sets but they wouldn't let us watch them. So everybody used to come to our house to watch t.v. My ol' man used to come home, cut the set off and just walk straight on through. And we'd all be sitting on the floor digging this and we knew better than to get up and turn the muthafucka back on. Best we get on out of there. It was time to get in the wind! That was some of the light shit he would pull.

He's an old type of negro dude in terms of what he thinks people should say, and that you should respect people who have position. That kind of thing. He still has that in his mind. I think inwardly he agrees with the Movement and all that. But when I talk to him, he'll tell me I shouldn't talk about the President like I do. I'm sure that it's the position he respects and not Johnson. My old man has been working at the same place for over thirty years. They gave him a medal. Dig it? But he's still a laborer. So now he's going to night school. He's got a good mind. But for negroes it will always be matter over mind.

He was never home. He'd come back from work and he'd split. He'd either go hunting or go out somewhere. His attitude toward white folks was they were wrong. He knew they were wrong, but he had the confidence that the law would take care of it, that it was a problem for the law. Although the white folks were doing us wrong, the good white folks were there, too. You know, like there's good and bad in every race.

I remember when the house behind ours caught fire and my ol' man made several trips inside it while it was burning, bringing people out. He got everybody out but a young baby he couldn't find. They gave him a medal for this too. They gave him this medal and put his picture in the paper. He was a hero and he knew everything was ready then. But the master trick that the muthafuckas pulled on him was that the bank sent him $1,000,000 worth of best wishes, so he was trying to figure out when they were gonna give him some money. He was really hung up over that shit. He was trying to convince himself that some whiteys might send him some dough 'cause he'd saved some other niggers. And they gave him a medal at Standard Oil, where he had been working for 30 fuckin years. Yeah, they gave him a medal. He was all-american. That's the way the psyche of our people works. Yeah, he had been in the burnin' house several times and they sent him $1,000,000 worth of best wishes. That's funny, you know. $1,000,000 dollars worth of best wishes. Explain that shit.

Watching my teachers and my old man did a lot toward shaping my thinking about what needed to be done in this country. At the same time this kind of thing was happening, I was also finding out about the white man. Once when I was young, we were coming back from across the river where

34

we had been visiting some relatives. It was raining and a cop pulled my old man over. I was about seven or eight at the time. I looked out the window and saw him and got down on the floor. He was a white cop, a cracker, and this was america. I was little, but somehow I knew then about white cops. This white cop started hollering and cursing at my old man in front of the whole family. And my old man hadn't done anything. So, I definitely had had my fill of cops after that.

I'd had experience with cops before, because they didn't want the Black kids to shoot off firecrackers at Christmas time. In the white community, you'd think there was a war going on, there'd be so many firecrackers going off. But they'd drive through the Black community to make sure we didn't shoot off none. We did anyway and would just run and hide when we saw the police car coming. But the point of their doing this was to instill fear of the police and of authority in us while we were still quite young.

When I was in the sixth grade there was this old white cop who used to patrol the corner right in front of the elementary school. One day at recess, I organized some little brothers to lay up on the hill and throw some rocks at him. And we bombed his ass. Some ol' negro lady across the street told the principal. I didn't even know she saw us. The principal called us in and beat us with a fan belt. Then she gave us notes to take home. Naturally, the notes told our parents what we'd done. "Well," I said, "I got to be a fool to take this note home to get another beating." So I threw mine away.

At that young an age, I was hostile toward white cops. That ol' white cop hadn't done nothing to us, but I didn't like him. There were a few white people in our community, and we didn't have anything against them. We used to play with the dudes. They all appeared to be slow learners.

That didn't last too long, though. One year when I was a cub scout, I went to the boy scout circus. I had on Ed's old uniform, so I was ready! It was held at the Coliseum on the Louisiana State University campus. In the back of the Coliseum they have the stalls where they keep the animals and this was where all the scout troops assembled. But there was a white section and there was our section. I was told that we shouldn't go around to the white section, because the crackers would shoot us with B.B. guns. "I ain't done nothing to the muthafuckas," I said, "and they ain't gon' shoot me. I'm going to go around there and see what's going on." So I went around there and as I was walking through one of the stalls, I heard a chump say, "Nigger! You have been sentenced to death!" And they started shooting with them B.B. guns. So I turned around and hauled ass getting out of there. I was climbing over a stall and I tore my pants. Right in the seat. A great big tear. My cub scout pants. My only cub scout pants! But I'm still getting up. I ain't stopped. I got back to our section, but I couldn't tell none of the brothers, because they'd told me not to go around there. So I decided I'd tell one of the white scoutmasters on them muthafuckas. I told one, "Mister, I went around there and the dudes shot me with a B.B. gun." The muthafucka looked at me and said, "Look here. Be a good sport about it, scout." Now how am I gon' be a good sport about getting shot? I realized then if I was going to get them muthafuckas back, I was gon' have to get 'em back on my own.

Well, the white troops always went out before us to entertain. So when they went out, I went back there and fucked up all their food. I peed in the tuna fish, spit in the potato salad, threw the hot dogs on the ground, stepped on the potato chips. I messed up everything. And the next year I brought by B.B. gun with me and I further fucked 'em up.

36

Them crackers had made me tear my only cub scout pants—right in the seat—and shot me too.

As if that wasn't enough, I had a confrontation with the police when I was going home. I was going home to take my pants off. The ol' blood scoutmaster had given me some tape to tape 'em up in the seat. I told him I'd torn 'em on a fence, 'cause I knew if I told him what I'd done, he would get mad at me for being around there. He gave me some masking tape. Some *white* masking tape to put on the seat of a pair of blue pants! And it was taped up like a big L right on the seat of the pants. So I said, hell, I'm going home, take these off, put on some regular clothes and come back later tonight. As I was walking home this cop car pulled up. I was young and his voice yelled out, "Hey, boy!" So I stopped and went over to the car and he said, "Where you going with your pants like that? Don't you know better than to be on the street wearing shit like that? You better get off the damn streets. Don't you never let me catch you out here with shit on like that again." After that I just decided to turn around and go back to the meeting. We didn't live more than a mile from LSU, but I didn't want to chance walking it after that. I thought I'd broke the law. My pants tore! It wasn't my fault, but I didn't know no better and I knew I better not say nothing to him or else I'd end up in jail.

I began to recognize then the value of being violent. I knew I hadn't done anything to make them white muthafuckas shoot their B.B. guns at me, so I knew that the world didn't run on love. The only thing that was gon' keep white muthafuckas off you was you!

The best example of that in the world today is america. America has made it clear that she respects only violence. When the rebellion went down in 1967 in Plainfield, New Jersey, the cops and the National Guard came into the Black community and were raising hell until the brothers sent word that they had guns. The cops and the Guard said, hell, them niggers got guns. We can't go over there and mess with 'em. America does not love China, but she refuses to move against China because she has the bomb. And all those troops. So what it means is that Black people have to address themselves to defending their communities and their homes, because if you can't defend them, you can't control them. Black folks got guns, but every time somebody says we're violent, Black people get up tight. Hell, we've been violent toward each other every Friday and Saturday night since there's been a Friday and Saturday night. Go to the emergency room of any hospital and see who they're bringing in on the weekend. The brother, and didn't no cracker shoot him.

Violence is accepted in america as long as it's white folks doing it. Turn on the t.v. and you go deaf from all the gunfire. Let two fighters get in the ring and let neither one of them hit the other and see what the real savages out there are going to do. They're going to scream for blood. It's no different than the people in ancient Rome who put lions on people.

So the question is not can Black people be violent. They send us to Vietnam and brag about what good fighters we are. It's legitimate for a Black man to go over there and kill 30 Vietcong and get a medal, but you come back here and kill one racist, red-necked, honky, camel-breathed peckerwood who's been misusing you and your people all your life and that's murder. That's homicide, because the white man has the power to define and legitimatize his actions. He can legitimatize violence. At this point we must address ourselves to defensive measures, something that will counteract that violence.

Violence also has a way of unifying a people. In the army

38

a camaraderie is always found among the guys in a regiment who've fought together. Years later when the dudes are fat, middle-aged men they get together and reminisce about all the "gooks" they killed and all the "enemy" chicks they screwed. One significant thing about Detroit and Newark was that the violence created a peoplehood. Black people had walked around under the illusion that they had a class system in the Black community. But the white man changed all that. He went in and beat "middle-class" as hard as lower-class Blacks. And "middle-class" Blacks were throwing as many fire bombs as the brother on the block. And afterwards, there was a real sense of community among the people, a real feeling of pride and togetherness. That came from the fact that they had fought together. It also came from the fact that they recognized that the honky cop kills Black people because they're Black. He doesn't put his gun away when he sees one in a suit or one who speaks so-called "good English." He will shoot just as many bullets at him as he does at the brother with a conk. So a peoplehood was forced upon Black people, through white violence.

The white man is our best teacher, up to a point. It was from watching white people, what they had, and what we had, that I learned about this country. I lived near Louisiana State University and I could see this big fine school with modern buildings and it was for whites. Then there was Southern University, which was about to fall in and that was for the niggers. And when I compared the two, the message that the white man was trying to get across was obvious. Nigger, you ain't shit. Die Nigger Die!

Negro america would do all sorts of ridiculous things to get close to that white world. I had an uncle who was supposed to be one of them big negroes and he used to go to LSU football games. One time he took me, because I dug football. We went down there and they had a little section for the niggers. A little section where the wind blew in. It seemed like they strategically located the niggers where the wind would blow right on 'em. It was a little fenced-off section and the negroes would sit there with cowbells and trumpets and act a fool for LSU. I sat there and froze. It was as cold as a witch's titty. I was cold and the game wasn't good. I'd seen better games at the blind school. But the negroes just sat there and enjoyed themselves. Later I found out that the real enjoyment was that they thought they was mingling with white folks. It was supposed to be big stuff to come down to white folks' games. But I said fuck that LSU game shit. I wasn't gon' sit there and freeze just so I could think I was mingling with white folks.

But that made me aware of where a whole lot of negroes was at. That was negro america again and it wasn't saying a thing. Negroes thought they were somebody, but all I had to do was look at the facilities LSU had and look at what Southern University had. The physical plant of LSU, even today, says the same thing it was saying when I was a kid—negroes ain't shit.

All of white america is a structure of institutions that says to Black people, "Nigger, you ain't shit." All standards of excellence, beauty, efficiency and civilization are such that any comparison between Black and white is designed to favor white and put down Black. And it's ground into a Black person every minute of every day, whether you're at work or whether you're out trying to have some fun, it's Nigger, you ain't shit. Die Nigger Die!

Then, if one examines negro institutions and community structures he finds the message is the same. Die Nigger Die!

Negro athletes run, jump and shuffle for white money as if to say, Die Nigger Die!

Negro politicians tell Black people to be nonviolent and patient and still they send Black people to jail, to make sure they die. However, after these politicians have been used, they will be next.

Negro entertainers sing "America is My Home," and play white roles on t.v. as if to say, "Let me help kill niggers."

Ebony, the negro *Life* magazine, the journal of negro culture, a "responsible" negro publication, raises the question, "Are Negro Women Getting Prettier?" while advertising for bleaching creams on the next page. Dye Nigger Dye!

Negro preachers steal money from poor Blacks on Sunday and drive Cadillacs all week. To the preacher money is God and he expects his God to travel with the poor.

Negro newspapers carry AP and UPI wire services. They steal misinformation from white nationalists and sell it to Black people, saying it's right 'cause it's white. Negro publications always oppose the Black liberation struggle until it is endorsed by whites. They speak to the needs of white people and never to Black people. *Jet* magazine, the cullard *Playboy*, a cross between a stag magazine and the *Pittsburg Police Gazette*, talks Black and sells white. These negroes, like whites, are all motivated by profit; money. But, "money won't change ya."

These attitudes assure the death of both negro and white america.

> Nigger, Nigger never die
> Shining face and bulging eyes!

I only vaguely remember my grandfather but somehow his life has shaped some of my thinking. He was my mother's father, I never knew my other grandfather. He was a kind old man, simple in manner with a small graying mustache and a face that proudly wore the imprints of time. He was a good, hardworking, churchgoing man who was always ready for a good fight and a good drink of whiskey. Papa, as he was affectionately called, spent all of his life in agriculture of one kind or another. He worked at the dairy at Louisiana State University and scraped together enough to build the little house we grew up in. He was the only grown man that I knew during that first period of my life because my father was away fighting for the land of the Ofay. The death of my grandfather did not come as a great shock to me because I was too young to understand death. I learned later that he died as a result of overwork. He worked himself to death. My mother would tell us stories about him and there is one that I will always remember. She told us that Papa worked for some rich white people in the evenings when he came from working at the dairy. During the depression they lost nearly everything they had. They asked my grandfather to continue to help them work the farm and, although they could not pay him at the time, promised to pay him a cumulative wage at a rate of $2.00 a day once they got on their feet. My grandfather worked that farm for 12 years. Once the farm became stable and the people recovered a lot of money they dismissed Papa without pay. He attempted to sue for the amount but the white lawyer said nothing could be done because there was no written contract. This story was my first encounter with flagrant injustice. I sensed that, for some reason I did not understand, the world was out of balance and that it rested disproportionately on the shoulders of Black people. My mother had to hold two jobs some of the time. She worked as a maid, taught at the orphanage home and then went to night school to try and get a better job. All that just to put us through school.

The first job I had was cutting grass for white folks. Ed and I used to cut acres of grass for two dollars. We'd finish that and they'd want us to trim the hedges and clean out the flower beds, all for $2.00. We did that for quite a few summers. And that whole concept of white people working Black people for nothing became very real to me, because I did it. In actuality, whites resent having to pay you anything, so they pay you as little as possible.

When I got to high school I had a job waiting tables in a night club. I worked three nights a week. One night I was waiting on these crackers and this cracker gave me a twenty-dollar bill and he thought he was giving me a five. But I was gon' to be honest and give him all his change. I gave it to him and he looked at me and frowned all up, as if to say, Nigger, you trying to be smart? That was the last time I played Reverend negro.

In the summers I did construction work. In other words, I was digging ditches. Couple of summers of that and I'd had enough of God's earth, so I got a job working on a ship. I was working from eight at night until eight the next morning for $1.00 an hour. What I was doing was cleaning the bottom of the ship out. You're so far down in the ship that you're in the part of the ship that's under water and it's hot as hell down there. Sometimes the ship would bring in oil and would be taking grain out, so you had to clean up all the oil. Everybody there was a brother except one little ol' young ass white boy. Naturally, they didn't put him down there with us. They had him goofing off up on the deck. He thought from that that he could tell us what to do. I wasn't buying that shit and I let him know right off he wasn't gon' say a damn thing to me. The dude in charge saw that I could influence the other brothers, because when I jumped bad, they jumped bad. So he decided he was gon' make me straw boss. Cut my work load, and my job would be to make the brothers work. What would happen was that we would go and hide. We would go climb some beams and cop some sleep and shit like that. So they needed somebody to make the brothers work and they wanted me for the job. I said, Cool. And I would *tell* the brothers to go sleep! Show 'em a good hiding place. I didn't give a shit.

The white boy soon saw that wasn't no more work getting done with me in charge, so he tried a new thing. He tried to get friendly with me. He was in charge of hiring and firing all the brothers who worked down there and I was working down there. But he tried to get friendly, telling me he remembered when he and I used to play football in City Park. I remembered. We used to whip their asses every week. We beat 'em once 106 to 6. And these were LSU's best football players. We used to kick their ass like ass-kicking was going out of style. So he tried to be buddy-buddy with me, but I wasn't buying that either.

One night he said something off-the-wall to one of the brothers and I told the brother to whup his ass. And the brother took that little white boy up on deck and picked him up and was about to throw him off the ship. Ninety feet above the water and he had this little cracker in his arms like he was a sack of rotten potatoes. I didn't say nothing. I was just standing there and digging it.

He didn't throw him off, though, but he scared the shit out of him. Well, soon as that little white boy got himself halfway back together he went and told some whiteys. And they came down and started talking bad to the brother who'd whupped the white boy. Then I jumped up and told 'em that we were ready to go to war any time they were and if they wasn't ready to go to war to shut the fuck up 'cause I was tired of all that damn talking. So a whole bunch of us got fired that night and I was happy to be rid of that job.

After that I got a job cleaning out petroleum tanks at one of the plants. That was a hellish job. Inside these storage tanks was steel webbing which was filled with concrete. When the concrete got corroded and contaminated by the

44

stuff being stored in there, it had to be chipped out with a chipping gun and that was my job. They gave me a 25-pound chipping gun and some eye goggles which wasn't as good as sunglasses and sent me down in these tanks to chip the concrete out from the webbing. And then after we'd chipped the stuff out, we had to fill the tanks with fresh concrete. And them tanks were about three stories high. That was my last job like that with whitey. I didn't know what I wanted to do, but I'd found out what I didn't want to be. I knew I didn't want to be a slave.

4

One of the basic problems any Black child has to deal with as he grows up is authority. First, there's the big white world that forces a white God and white Jesus on him and has him worshipping somebody that doesn't even look like him. There's that big white world telling him what's right and what's wrong and how to do and how not to do and all of it is designed to keep him oppressed, to keep him down. And all of that is reinforced by negro america, which is a mirror of the big white world and does the white world's job inside the Black community. Negro america becomes the official policeman for white america. You grow up and you're taught not to talk back to white people, not to look at white women, to be respectful, to speak so-called correct English, to grease and straighten your hair, to scrub your skin as white as you can.

At some point or another, the Black child begins to challenge this authority, both within negro america and the big white world when he confronts it. Some Black people rebel like J.S. and become so-called criminals. He declared war on that authority, but his weapons were inadequate.

My rebellion against this authority occurred whenever I encountered negro america. When I entered Southern University in 1960, I was fifteen years old. I was in constant conflict with the administration. It was really like a plantation. The Presidency had been handed down from the father to the son, who should've died with his father. He was truly a white man's boy and didn't mind folks knowing it. This nigger was so bad, he powdered his face.

One time I remember Odetta came to do a concert. We

were required to wear suits and ties to concerts and things like that. So we got all knotted up and went down and here came these white dudes from LSU with sport shirts and sneakers on. I stopped right at the door and started screaming and hollering on the Dean who was standing there. "Man, what's wrong with you? How you gon' let them boys in there?" But he pretended like he hadn't seen them white boys. "You saw it!" I yelled. "Don't come handing me that." I was making so much racket that he told me to meet him in his office the next day. I went and before he could say a word, I jumped down his throat again. I called him a whole bunch of names and he got mad and threatened to kick me out of school.

That showed me again where negro america was. They were scared not to love white people. He come trying to tell me, "Well, if they went in with sneakers on, that just shows their ignorance." I said, "Man, don't come telling me that. You could put on a tie and the finest suit in the world and they wouldn't let you in a concert at LSU. Don't run nothing like that down on me. Telling me that's their ignorance. That's your ignorance, muthafucka!"

Here was that question of authority again. If authority is to be used, it should not be a coercive type thing. After all, what dictates that a person can be put in an authoritative position over someone else? If it's experience, then respect should come from that, not authority. People should adhere to rules because they respect them and not because some position mandates that respect. Now if you raise a legitimate issue with a person and they respect it, then they're gonna adhere to it. It's like the principle of self-determination. But when you're in a certain position and you tell a cat to do something with no grounds for it, it provokes a type of rebellious behavior.

This occurs throughout america. In negro america, any-

thing the teacher or the preacher or the doctor says is law. Not because it's right, but because of who said it. In white america, if the President or Senator Dipshit says it, no one challenges it. It can be wrong as hell, but everybody applauds anyway. I don't give a shit who says what. If the muthafucka is wrong, he's wrong.

My rebellion in its early stages was against authority which did nothing against the authority which was in charge of negroes—the white folks. Teachers, for example. I didn't respect 'em because I knew how they were around white folks. I didn't understand and still don't understand why people are so insecure that they can't talk out against certain things. If something didn't go right, they'd just lay back and say, "Well, it'll get better and things will improve. Ain't nothing I can do about it; it'll better itself." "The Lawd will fix it."

In this country, authority is a cover for wrong. I don't respect wrong and I don't respect authority that represents wrong. And old cracker ass Lightning Bug Johnson knows that's true, because I told him myself. Back in 1965, I was living in Washington, D.C., and I was Chairman of NAG, the Non-Violent Action Group. It was the time of the Selma March when people were beaten up on Pettis Bridge. We had a delegation to go to see Johnson. First we went to see Katzenbach. A negro minister said we don't want to take too many 'cause we don't want him to feel threatened. Katzenbach assumed the typical white attitude. I remember Lester McKinney was trying to raise a question and Katzenbach ignored him. So, I told Katzenbach that if he couldn't answer the man's question, then I didn't see what we were doing there.

The following day we were supposed to go see Humphrey, but we never did. The next day we went to see Johnson in this big conference room that had this conference

51

table about two miles long. About 20 members comprised the delegation, white and negro. When we went in, everybody sat down and then Johnson came in. From the jump, the leader of the delegation who is now one of the boys in charge of Washington D.C., went into his act. Soon as "the man" got there, he started grinning and laughing. He had this statement written out and he passed it across the table to Johnson. Johnson was arrogant as hell and mad 'cause we were there. His whole attitude was, "What you niggers doin' here takin' up my time." He pissed me off from the get. Well, he looked at the statement and didn't even read it. He just threw it back across the table. Threw it back! And this negro reached out and picked it up. Now if I'd been sitting next to this negro, I would've picked it up and thrown it back at that cracker and we would've had a war right there. But he took it.

After that, each member of the delegation introduced himself and said a few words. The dude from the NAACP got up and said, "Mr. President, it really is a pleasure to be here. This will be something that I'll be proud to tell my children and grandchildren about." Then came another fool and he said the same thing. Next came the dude from CORE and I thought, Well, I know he's supposed to be a militant, a bad dude, and he's gonna tell this cracker what's on his mind. He got up and said, "Good morning, Mr. President. It is a pleasure to be here."

Well, it was my time and I'm really pissed off by this time. It was obvious that everyone was tommin' and nobody was going to speak to the issue. So I started off by telling Johnson, "I'm not happy to be here and I think it's unnecessary that we have to be here protesting against the brutality that Black people are subjected to. And furthermore, I think that the majority of Black people that voted for you wish that they had gone fishing." While our negro leader had been talking about civil rights, Johnson had cut in on him and said, "Speaking of deprivation of rights, my two daughters couldn't sleep last night because of all that picketing noise out in front of the White House." So I told him, "I don't think anyone is interested in whether your daughters could sleep or not. We are interested in the lives of our people. Which side is the federal government on?" I looked around and the bootlickers were getting scared. Man, negroes were getting scared. Johnson's whole attitude changed.

The next day Drew Pearson (one of the many white authorities on negroes) said that I had treated Johnson with "ill abuse." But once Johnson's attitude changed it was easier then for other dudes to begin to talk. But the negroes still didn't raise the points that they should've. There were two white cats who halfway tore into Johnson's ass. When we came out, all them jive Toms and all them old white folks come running round telling me what a good job I had done and that it was good that I had done that. Those are the kind of friends you don't need!

To me, Johnson was a dude who used his position against people and I can't buy that. It's ridiculous. The President ain't nothing but another man. And Johnson was a big-eared, ugly, red-necked cracker. I looked at that muthafucka's ears. If he could learn to wiggle them he could fly. I ain't bullshitting. And when I was tearing into Johnson's ass, Humphrey, who is supposed to be a "liberal," was getting madder than a pimp with dogshit on his shoe. So, I looked at him and knew where he was at. The little red punk.

And to show the muthafuckas what I thought about the whole meeting, I stole some stuff out of the White House. I liberated everything I could! Sure did. Show you what I think of you, muthafuckas. I was trying to figure how to get a painting off the wall and put it under my coat. I figured it belonged to me anyway.

The whole concept of authority has to be redefined. People have to understand that individuals, not positions, merit respect. Negro america and white america assume that positions mandate respect. When this respect for position does not materialize, they begin to utilize force. This is why the Black world has rejected both negro america and white america and their ideas of authority.

5 The biggest difference between being known as a Black man or a negro is that if you're Black, then you do everything you can to fight white folks. If you're negro, you do everything you can to appease them. If you're Black, you're constantly in and out of trouble, because you're always messing with "the man." If white folks say it's more cultured to whisper, you talk loud. If white folks say gray suits are fashionable, you go buy a pink one. If they say america is great, you say america ain't shit. Chairman Mao says, "Whatever the enemy supports, we oppose. Whatever the enemy opposes, we support." I hadn't read Chairman Mao when I was in high school, but I already understood that fundamental revolutionary principle. I knew white folks couldn't do wrong right, so whatever they thought was good, I knew wasn't.

A lot of people, Black and white, have the impression that those of us who got involved in the Movement, when it started in 1960, were fighting for integration. That's the way the white press interpreted the sit-ins and freedom rides and all that. But what they didn't understand was that none of us was concerned about sitting down next to a white man and eating a hamburger. Anybody who thinks that is reflecting white nationalism. That's that white supremacist attitude. Nothing is good unless it can be done in the company of white people. We would've been some kind of fools to get beaten up, spat on and jailed the way a lot of folks did just to sit down at a lunch counter beside a white person. Integration was never our concern. In fact, integration is impractical. You cannot legislate an attitude and integration is based upon an attitude of mutual acceptance and respect between two racial or cultural groups in the society. A law can govern behavior, but attitudes cannot be forced or enforced, and what the Civil Rights Movement was concerned with was controlling the animalistic *behavior* of white people. I resented somebody telling me I couldn't eat at a certain place. It wasn't that I wanted to eat there. Hell no! I always knew we had the best food anyway. But as part of that constant battle waged by Black people against white america, if white folks didn't want me to eat there, in the door I went. If I had a free choice, I'd sit in the back of the bus. That's where the heater is. We weren't fighting for integration. We were letting white folks know that they could no longer legislate where we went or what we did.

Every Black person belongs to the Movement, whether he's been on a demonstration or not. The lives of Black people are political, because Black people carry on a constant war against "the man." So I was political, even before I knew the word, but it wasn't until I got into high school that I became involved in more overt political activities.

I got involved in the Movement through my brother Ed. Ever since he was a little boy, he'd been in and out of things folks thought he shouldn't have been in. He wanted to do things on his own. But some of the things he's done! He's caused the family some trouble. One time he put a firecracker in his ear and asked me did I believe he would light it. Naturally I told him, no. It was Christmas Eve. I was about eight and Ed was ten. Well, he said he was goin' to light it and then grab it and throw it out the window. He lit it, and just as he grabbed it, it exploded. They had to call the doctor for the blood on Christmas Eve. Another time, the lady next door had a wringer-type washing machine. We were in the house and we heard somebody screaming and hollering and we looked over there and Ed had his arm halfway in the wringer. He had put his fingers in there, teasing the machine, putting them in and pulling them out. The machine caught one finger and pulled his arm all the way up to his elbow and broke some of the bones in his finger and part of his arm. And that muthafucka moaned. I ain't never heard a muthafucka moan like that in my life. And I laughed. I sure did. They put him on the bed and he moaned like he was dying. Ed was one of them kind of dudes who'd write his last will and testament every time he'd get sick. He'd get a piece of paper and will me his bicycle, which I never got. Ed was also a dude who was always losing stuff. He went to boy scout camp one summer and my ol' lady bought him all kinds of new stuff to take to camp. Well, on the last day of camp we saw Ed walking up the hill with a blanket on his back. When Ed opened the blanket, he didn't have nothing but a piece of driftwood, one tennis shoe and a whole blanketful of red mud. He'd lost his camping equipment, his brand new shoes, hatchet and everything. All he didn't lose he had gambled away.

Yea, he's my main nigger. He was the first one in the family to go to jail. He was twelve the first time he got arrested. There were poor white folks living down the street from us. It wasn't important that they were poor, but that they were white. That was what they always emphasized. And that's the reason poor Blacks and whites in the South can't get together. Poor white folks will always let you know that even though they're ignorant, hungry and dirty, they're white and that makes them better than niggers. As long as they got that attiude, I don't want nobody talking to me about coalitions with poor whites.

Well, one day Ed and a bunch of us were skating down the street in front of where these poor crackers lived. They came out and said we couldn't skate down there, 'cause it made too much noise. They just did it 'cause we were bloods. If it'd been white kids skating, they would've liked the noise. Anyway, we told 'em they didn't own the sidewalk and if they couldn't stand the noise, put some cotton in their ears or move out of the neighborhood. We really didn't care. Well, they went and called the police. So everybody split, everybody except Ed. He just stood there and woofed at the police, talking about their mamas and shit like that. You know a blood. Play the Dozens in a minute. Naturally, ain't no white cop gon' take that kind of shit off no nigger, so they put Ed in the car and took him down. My old man had to go down and get him.

The second time he got arrested, they accused him of staring at a white girl in a house down the street. He had gone down there to see a friend of ours and some white folks called the police on him. That's another example of how white folks think they're superior. They just naturally assume that white women are better-looking and that every Black man wants one. Black people have never said a word on the subject. It's always white folks talking all that trash about niggers wanting white women. What makes them think that a white woman is a queen or some shit like that? Hell, if Ed had been staring at the bitch, they should've thanked him for doing the bitch a favor.

The next time he got arrested was when he was in college. He was in the first sit-ins at Southern University and got expelled. From then on he was political. After he got expelled, he got a scholarship to Howard University from some people who had hustled up some dough.

I got involved in the Movement two years later. In the spring of 1960, there were some demonstrations going on at the Southern University campus and my high school class marched up on campus to a meeting that they were having.

58

And as a result the whole class was put out of school for two days. From then on, I used to stay in close contact with Ed and he started telling me about NAG, a group centered around students from Howard that did a lot of work around the Washington, D.C., community. Ed was in it at the time with a lot of people who later got with SNCC—Stokely, Courtland Cox, Mary Lovelace, Muriel Tillinghast and the whole Howard crew. So in '62 I started spending my summers in D.C. with Ed.

The first day I got there NAG had Ed on a picket line out in front of National Shirt Shop. I sure didn't feel like walking, but you know, we stayed out there. That was a good summer, because I really began to relate to Black problems as the problems of a group and not individuals. I read DuBois, Frederick Douglass, Marcus Garvey, Richard Wright. Plus, I attended a lot of meetings in D.C. where brothers talked some heavy shit and I could just catch some of the things they were saying 'cause I hadn't read all the books. I mean they were talking some shit. I hadn't ever heard niggers talk no shit like this before. Damn! So I'd sit there and listen. Nearly the whole summer I'd be listening and reading. That was when I met Stanley Wise, who a few years later was elected Executive Secretary of SNCC at the time I was elected Chairman. And Wise was truly a wild blood. He was Chairman of NAG at the time and he'd be conducting meetings. I met Eric Jones at that time, too, and he later worked with me in Alabama. When I went back to school the dudes couldn't tell me nothing, 'cause, like, they hadn't read what I'd been reading or heard what I'd been hearing.

I went back to D.C. the next summer, the summer of 1963. This was during the Cambridge thing and I went over to Cambridge with Courtland Cox, who had become Program Secretary of SNCC. Courtland told me we would just go down to Cambridge for the day and come back that night. We went over there and spent a week. Courtland was a person who never had a concept of time or money. He would spend money like it was going out of style. They called him "Sky King." This was when SNCC was prosperous..

We were working with the people, organizing, going to meetings. I still was just listening. I wasn't doing any talking. I always had a lot to say, but apart from playing the Dozens, I hadn't been accustomed to talking out in public —it's not something you just jump up and do. I'd discuss things later with Ed, and bring out some points, but I just wouldn't get up and talk.

The following summer, SNCC organized the Mississippi Summer Project. This was the summer when hundreds of white college students came into Mississippi and the summer that James Chaney, Michael Schwerner and Andrew Goodman were murdered. I went down to Holmes County and stayed about four weeks and then went up to D.C. I'd decided not to go back to Southern University in the fall, so I left Mississippi early to go to see about some kind of job in D.C.

At the end of the summer, I went over to Atlantic City for the Democratic Convention and the challenge by the Mississippi Freedom Democratic Party. The challenge was very significant because it made us realize that the whole conspiracy was not just a conspiracy of the South. It was a conspiracy of the nation when the Democratic Party refused to seat the MFDP, which was perfectly correct when it said that the Mississippi delegation to the Convention did not represent the people of Mississippi. But the Democratic Party wasn't hearing that, because Eastland and Stennis had a whole lot of power in the Senate. Black people be damned! And the white liberals like Walter Reuther, Joe Rauh, Humphrey and all of them folks went along with the thing. And these were the dudes who were supposed to be on our side. They tried to sell the MFDP out and get them to accept two seats, give them token recognition. But the MFDP wouldn't hear it. So all the liberals, our "friends," turned against us.

Folks never want to believe that kind of shit. Like even when you were down South and something happened, you'd call the FBI and they'd come out there and trick you into believing that they were going to see that you got some justice. You had to believe them because they represented the federal government. And you didn't want to face the fact that the federal government wasn't on your side. Well, we found out. Bobby Kennedy was Attorney General and folks don't want to believe it, but he did not come to the aid of the civil rights workers. In Albany, Georgia, the federal government had civil rights workers arrested and tried because a cracker said they were hurting his business. In Mississippi, civil rights workers were killed, because Bobby Kennedy said the federal government couldn't protect them. In Alabama, civil rights workers were killed and the federal government wouldn't move against Wallace. And yet negroes cried over the Kennedys worse than they would've cried over their own mamas. The Kennedys didn't do anything for the rights of Black people, but because they talked like they cared, negroes fell for what they said like a bunch of chumps. When John Kennedy had a chance to appoint a federal judge in Mississippi who would knock down some of those racist laws, he appointed a cracker pig racist named Cox. That showed how much he thought of Black people. John and Bobby Kennedy were enemies of Black people, but negroes were more upset when John Kennedy was killed than they were when Malcolm X was killed. In fact, negroes hated Malcolm because when

John Kennedy was killed, Malcolm said, "The chickens are coming home to roost." Now, everybody talks about Malcolm like they loved him so much when he was alive, but that's a lie and they know it. When Malcolm was killed, the majority of negroes reacted the same way white people did. They were glad, because they had been told that Malcolm was going around stirring up trouble. Negroes have a hard time accepting anything Black unless it's been legitimatized by white people. John Kennedy was legitimate. Malcolm was not. If the white man was to package horseshit, put a name on it and advertise it on t.v., "Barbecued Horseshit," negroes would go buy it, because the white man said it was good. But that's the way it's going to be as long as white people have the power. Anything you don't control is a weapon against you. And as long as Black people are unable to control, Willie Mays will never be the greatest baseball player who ever lived. It will always be Babe Ruth. Bob Cousey will always be the greatest basketball player and not Bill Russell or Oscar Robertson. And O. J. knows better than anybody that it's always going to be a white boy that's the greatest football player. Black people have to understand that everything in this country is political.

The MFDP challenge not only pointed up the total lack of power Black people had, but it also showed that even when you're right, you lose. Black people in Mississippi had a legitimate grievance. They had no representation in the government. They came to the Democratic Convention and the federal government seeking a redress of that grievance and they were offered two token seats in the Convention. The Convention was a classic example of the lack of a vehicle for the redress of grievances for Black people. We don't have any machinery to talk about the denial of justice. The anti-war movement now recognizes what Black people have learned. Johnson was elected in 1964 because he said

that Asian boys (you dig him calling grown men "boys"?)
should fight an Asian war. And Johnson got the biggest
popular vote in american history and proceeded to fight the
war like he was defending ol' ugly Ladybird from an attack. He did not recognize the popular vote. He recognized
the Democratic Party. And it should be clear to all by now
that there is no difference between the Democratic and
Republican parties. There's only one party in america and
that's the party of white nationalism. Both parties have
made it clear that they will not tolerate dissent from Blacks
or from whites. And even if they did tolerate dissent, it
wouldn't mean a damn thing, because dissent does not
change policy. A hundred thousand people went to the
Pentagon, and Johnson escalated the war. People took over
the streets of Chicago and the Democratic Party nominated
Hump the Dump. When the people cannot find a redress of
their grievances within a system, they have no choice but
to destroy the system which is responsible in the first place
for their grievances. The government is the lawbreaker. The
people must become the law enforcer. We cannot allow the
government to be an outlaw, particularly when the crime is
against the people.

6

In the fall of 1964, after the MFDP challenge in Atlantic City, I returned to D.C. and got a job working down at the library in the Department of Agriculture. Rap Brown, GS-2! Dig that! My supervisor was this white cracker bitch from New Orleans. Well, I ain't never been too hip on punching time clocks and going through all them kind of changes, so anytime I could get leave—sick leave, bathroom leave, any kind of leave— I'd leave. I'd split to Atlanta where SNCC's national office is. I was just about commuting between Atlanta and D.C., I took so much leave.

I had gotten the library job through a friend of mine, James Dillday, who was working down there. He was a good blood. He used to take all the napkins out of the containers in the cafeteria and write "Freedom Now," and "We Shall Overcome" on 'em. Then he'd put 'em back in the containers and lay back and watch the white folks when they pulled out a napkin.

I knew when I got the job that I wasn't going to be there long. They would get pissed off at me 'cause I'd wear my black denim jacket and tennis shoes to work. So they called me in about it and I told 'em I didn't have no white collar job and I wasn't gon' be putting on no tie to push goddam baskets up and down the hall. (That's all I did—stamped books and carried 'em from one place to another.) Well, they didn't dig that too much, plus I was wearing my hair long.

I stayed for about three months and at Christmas time I split for Baton Rouge. I had saved up three days' leave and

I'd figured it all out how I'd go home and just stay down there and call in for leave without pay. When I got back, they got this negro to call me in and tell me that I had been missing too much time. So I said, well, it's my leave and I don't want to save it. It's my leave. I earned it. The dude allowed as to how that was true, but he thought it would be best if I got me another job. I said, Solid, and resigned.

All that fall, I'd been working with the Howard people in NAG and I was elected Chairman. Even though I never went to Howard myself, I wanted to develop the relationship between the school and the community. The negro university has always been set apart, across the tracks from the Black community. That's part of the divide-and-conquer strategy of white folks. If you can make the Black university students seem like they're different and better than, say, what they call the "block boys," then you can keep 'em confused and fighting. At Howard, people would always be talking about how bad the "block boys" were. I never had any trouble with the brothers, and I couldn't understand the attitude of the Howard students. I couldn't see why you had to be scared of each other—why you had to be scared of other Black people.

I saw my role as one of trying to get college students to identify with the brothers in the street. (And you didn't have to have any other reason than developing some security for yourself when you left campus. Do it so you could feel safe to walk out there among them.)

Negro college students have always felt themselves to be better than the brother on the block. Naturally, the brother would resent this and the first chance he got, he was upside the college student's head. That situation can only be overcome by the college student taking the initiative in overcoming whatever split might exist between himself and the blood on the corner. College students, however, get caught in a trick, because they think that to be accepted by the young bloods, they have to be tough, be a warrior. But all they have to do is show the brother that they respect him and that they recognize that he is a brother. All Black people are involved in the same struggle. Revolutionaries are not necessarily born poor or in the ghetto. There is a role for every person in revolution if he is revolutionary. You don't have to throw a Molotov cocktail to be a revolutionary. One thing which the Black college student can do is to begin to legitimatize the brother's actions—begin to articulate his position, because the college student has the skills that the blood doesn't have. It reminds me of the old story about the father and his son. The son comes to the father and says, "You told me that the lion was the king of the jungle. Yet in every story I read, the man always beats the lion. Why is that?" The father looks at the son and says, "Son, the story will always end the same until the lion learns how to write." If you don't begin to tell your own story, you will always be Aunt Jemima; you will always be "rioting." You must begin to articulate a position of your own.

The Black college student, if he is revolutionary, can help Black people to purge themselves of the misinformation that they've been fed all their lives. White nationalism has been instilled into us whether we know it or not. We have been told that George Washington should be our hero. George Washington is no hero of Blacks. He had 13 children and none by Martha. They were slaves. They tell us we should celebrate Christopher Columbus' birthday. Christopher Columbus was a 15th-century Eisenhower. He was so dumb. He was trying to get to India. Did you ever see where India is on the map? But america has the power to legitimatize these people and make them heroes in our minds. America has negroes in the dilemma of thinking that everything Black is bad. Black cows don't give good milk; black

67

hens don't lay eggs; black mail is bad; you wear black to funerals, white to weddings; angel food cake is white, devil's food cake is black. And all good guys wear white hats. And Black people fall for it. Everything Black is bad. That's white nationalism. And they tell you, you can't talk about Black nationalism. So how do you combat it if you grow up telling your children you should respect Santa Claus. Come December 25th Santa Claus is so white that he slides down a black chimney and comes out white. But you tell your children that Santa Claus brought those toys and you take them to see a white Santa Claus. So therefore, it becomes instilled in their minds that Santa Claus is good because Santa Claus is white. Thus, we help foster that type of white nationalism. You must begin to define for yourself; you must begin to define your Black heritage. You must begin to investigate and learn on your own. They will never tell you that Hannibal was Black. They'll never tell you that African societies back in the 16th century were the most modern known at that time and that the highest degree of culture existed there. Every time you open a book here in America, they gonna show you Uncle Tom's cabin or they gonna show you Double-O Soul with a piece of watermelon. It becomes the responsibility of the Black college student to combat this sort of thing. The education that a Black college student gets will be irrelevant, fruitless and worthless unless he uses it to define and articulate positions that are relevant to Black people. It does you no good to come to school and pledge to cross the burning sand. Hell, you ain't never got off the burning sand! Pledging is no good for Black people in america. When "the man" moves against you, your Omega sticker does not mean that he is going to pass you by. All it means is that he might take you to a different camp. If you must pledge, pledge to be a revolutionary. You are involved in the struggle whether you want to be or not. Your badge of involvement is your skin. Therefore, you got to quit walking around talking about those people out there acting crazy. Them!! That's you!! Anything we do will have a profound impact on you.

These were some of the things I learned and tried to work out while I was Chairman of NAG, trying to ease the tensions that existed between the college students and the brothers on the block. It was while I was working with NAG that I had the meeting at the White House with Johnson, which I mentioned earlier. A short time after that, I got this letter from my draft board. Now I ain't saying that there's any connection between the two, but that's the way the deal went down.

Well, when I went down to Baltimore for my physical, I raised so much hell, they told me that I couldn't even volunteer. I talked about one dude's mama so bad, it hurt *me*! They sent me to every doctor there. When they'd ask, Can you do deep knee bends, I'd say "No." When they'd ask, Can you raise your right shoulder, I'd throw my right arm up in the air and say "No." Anything they asked, I said "No." Loud and clear! "No."

I started raising hell the minute I hit the army base. I was pissed off that I even had to go over there. When I got off the bus I had all my human rights and "Fuck your Mama" buttons on and I was ready! So I got off the bus and was walking down the middle of the street. I wouldn't get out of the street and this army truck came up behind me and was trying to get through and here's The Rap walking down the middle of the street. And I wouldn't let him get past. So when I turned to go into this building, he pulled up beside me and said, "Hey buddy, I . . ." I said, "I ain't your buddy! I don't know you!" And I kept walking. I didn't know I was going to see that muthafucka again. So I went on down to the building where everybody was to assemble. While we were sitting

there, this army dude screamed at one of the bloods who had his cap on. At that time all the block bloods wore little caps and you just didn't take your cap off for nothing or nobody. When he screamed at the brother to take his damn hat off, I screamed back: "Cut out all that goddam hollering!" The dude turned in my direction, but he didn't know who had said it. So he threw another brother out of the room. When the cat was going out, I jumped up and said, "What's wrong? You must be dumb or something. It wasn't him. It was me." So he told me to get out. I told him, "I'll be glad to get out. I didn't want to come."

I went on downstairs and then I dug that the cat had no intention of letting me come back that day, which meant I'd have to come back another day. So I went back upstairs and stood before the whole group and started screaming on the fool. I told him, "Show me where headquarters is. I'll get this shit straightened out." He said he would take me there. Well, that was going to blow my game, 'cause I'd planned to lie on the muthafucka, say that he was discriminating against me 'cause I had on SNCC buttons (and I figured he was), but he only took me far enough to point it out to me.

I went in there and asked for the Commander. He wasn't in, but they gave me the dude under him. And guess who it was? The dude who had been driving the truck. He came over to me and said, "Ain't you the one that was walking in the street today?" I said, "Yeah, I'm the one! What about it?" I was in the shit then and had to play that bad game. So I went on and told him I'd come to see about why they were discriminating against me because I had on SNCC buttons. So the cat called back over there and told 'em to let me go ahead and take the exams. So I went on back and I was bad, 'cause I'd screamed on this fool in front of all the brothers and shit. When I came back in, they started cheering. But the dude assigned me number 100 to make me last.

Well, I had a good thing going and they were about to write me off. There were three questions on the form that I'd refused to answer. I'd talked to some of the brothers ahead of time and they'd told me to leave three questions blank: Are you addicted to drugs? Are you an excessive drinker? Do you have homosexual tendencies? The doctor was about to write me off and he hadn't even noticed that I'd left these questions blank. I didn't want to blow my thing, so I kinda pointed that out to him. He said that was O.K.

I went on back over to the big building. When I got there, they'd received a call to have me sent back over to the doctors. So I went back and they sent me to a bunch of them all the way up to the head one. All this time they'd been trying to make me fill out those three questions and I wouldn't. So the head guy, a cracker named Lt. Casper, was supposed to be bad and he was going to MAKE me fill it out. Well, he started woofing. I jumped on him so bad all the brothers started gathering around the door. I talked about his mama like a dog and then jumped up and started out the door. He said, "Where're you going?" I said, "I'm going to headquarters." Yeah, I was gon' go back to headquarters and tell some more lies on them muthafuckas.

I went on back over there and talked to somebody else this time. I told him that Casper had said he was going to recommend that I be drafted immediately, that he had erased all my ailments from the form and shit like that. When I left headquarters I stuck my head in Casper's office and yelled, "You and your grainy-mouthed mama will be in Vietnam before me." He told a white fellow, "That's one of them smart niggers."

The next time they called me down, they sent me through fast. Anything I said was wrong with me, they said yes to.

"Yeah, you got bad feet. Yeah, you got a bad shoulder. Anything else wrong?" They didn't want me. I'd already told 'em that if they gave me a gun and told me to shoot my enemy, I'd shoot Ladybird. If sanity is dropping bombs on humans, then thank goodness for insanity.

7

After I left the Department of Agriculture, I got a job with the poverty program as a neighborhood worker and that's really when I began to see where "the man" was at. The poverty program was designed to take those people whom the government considered threatening to the structure and buy them off. It didn't address itself to the causes of poverty but to the effects of poverty. But we tried to do something with it. We had some young cats and we had some poor people in the program, but we really weren't the controlling force. What controlled the poverty program was money. They'd play dudes off against each other by promising one more money than the other and all that kind of thing. It was the whole trick of the stick and the carrot in front of the mule. If you do a better job than this other dude, then you get this carrot. There were cats who were really hustling for that, but it didn't make me no difference, 'cause I didn't plan to stay there that long. I don't hustle against other people for that money thing. You got negroes going around now talking about Green Power is better than Black Power. As long as america has the power to change the color of money, then money don't mean a thing. Negroes yelling Green Power and they gon' look up one day and "the man" is going to tell them that red money is the only good money this week. There is no solution in money. "Power comes from the barrel of a gun," like Mao said, and not from the size of your bank account.

The poverty program was an example of the government trying to use a little Green Power to buy people off. It attracted some really good people who would diligently walk those streets trying to organize people, but they didn't have nothing to offer them. Frustration began to set in early. And people began to see how fruitless that type of work was. People would come up with really good ideas, too.

Gaston Neal, who now heads up the New School of Afro-American Thought in D.C., was training at the same time I was. He came up with the idea of an arts festival to get all the people together. So he got all the local talent from D.C. to participate in the show. Well, along comes Voice of America saying that they want to tape it. Naturally, Neal tells them, "Hell no, you can't tape the show." And that was the correct position. Don't let the muthafucking crackers tape nothing. They just wanted to use it as propaganda in Africa, to try and show how happy we all are with all this freedom and democracy they got here in this country, and we know that's a crock of shit.

Well, after he told them they couldn't tape the show, they went down to tell the head of the D.C. poverty program. Neal came to get me. The head of the program was a negro of the highest order—a colored man as loyal to his masters as a dog. So he says, "Well, you gotta let them tape the show." Neal seemed to have a fear of authority and he let that negro and his white masters, who were also there, woof him down. They was just there to make sure the nigger said the right things and to jack his ass up if he didn't.

Well, I jumped up and said, "Hell no. The man said you can't tape the show and that means you can't tape it." The Voice of America muthafucka looked at me and I said, "That's right, you can't tape the show." This was right after Watts.

Then the muthafucka went into his white psyche thing and come on with all this jive about how it was gonna be played overseas. I said, "Well, why don't you go on and tape what's happening in Watts and play it overseas, if you wanna play something?" I said, "The Voice of America is a right-wing cracker organization." I ran it down on that chump. Neal and the others started getting their confidence back again and they started saying things to him.

The next trick they pulled was to say that we couldn't have the show at all. Neal kinda looked off 'cause he didn't want to see all the work he'd been doing going to waste. So I said, "Well, call it off." I knew damned well that they weren't going to call it off 'cause dudes had already passed tickets out all over the community and I knew the folks would tear the place down. I called their bluff and the dudes backed down. They didn't want to talk to me no more. They wanted to get Neal off to the side. I said, "Hell no. If you can't talk to all of us, then you can't talk to none of us."

That was one of the few power plays that we utilized. I got away with a whole lot of shit because I had a base in the community, plus all the local people in the program supported me. I started organizing a union. But the people from the downtown program began to infiltrate it and tried to disrupt it, by talking about, "Let's not have a union; let's have an association." That was shitless. It didn't have any force. I was trying to organize neighborhood workers. This would really create a power base to determine who was to be hired, who was to be fired and what kind of salaries would be paid. But the thing got sidetracked into this whole association thing.

But I guess because I'd tried to form a union, I became a marked man down on the books at the main office. So they tried to buy me off and give me a job up there. I went up to get interviewed. I thought I would fool with the muthafuckas a little, 'cause I didn't want that kind of a job. I went to work when I got ready. I came home to sleep when I got ready. What did I want with a job up there?

So I continued working in the community until this whole

77

police-community relations thing came up. You know. The police should have better relations with the community and the community should realize that the policeman is their friend and all that shit. I got switched to the police-community relations program, which was O.K. with me 'cause I wanted to jack up the police anyway.

Well, they began setting up meetings between the community and the police. The police came in there with that white attitude. So I used to just rip their ass. Colored cops and white cops. They told me to come over to the precinct and talk to the Captain. I went on over there and the cracker was trying to get *me* to be a policeman. I told him I wasn't interested and I had a record. He said, "Oh, that's O.K. That's O.K." I told him that I just wasn't interested. So he said, "We'll get you for a policeman before it's over. We'll get you." That was as much proof as I needed to know that them muthafuckas was crazy. Rap Brown, policeman! Get to that!

I went over there one other time to talk with this Captain about the police messing with some people. I told him that the community was about to explode if he didn't do certain things. I told him that we'd unleash the people on his ass. So they started doing things like integrating patrol cars. It really showed me how much the structure feared our community and that the strength really lies in that community. The cops ain't worth shit if a million muthafuckas decide to kick their ass. Some cops obviously know that but it's them dumb cops that they don't discipline or restrain—the cracker cops from North Carolina, Virginia, Mississippi and Alabama. But we must understand that the cops are not the only problem. Cops serve the system, just like the army in Vietnam. The system allows cops to be what they are. In D.C., they recruit actively down south for policemen. Most of the negro cops in D.C. have a high school degree and two or three years of college, while the white cops don't even finish high school. But the people with position are white cops—all the way down the line. Out of the 16 or 17 precincts in Black D.C., they had one negro Captain, seven negro Lieutenants, 13 or 14 Sergeants in a police force of some 5,000 odd men. So I would attack the chumps on that.

The poverty program was an experience in terms of what the government was gonna do and what they were capable of doing, because it was nothing more than a way to buy off certain people. It never dealt with the causes of poverty. I came to the conclusion that this just ain't it. One day when the Director told us to go from house to house and get people's names on a list, I finally split. I wasn't for that! That wasn't organizing and I told him so. He said, "Well, this is what you're going to do." So everybody went out and they were bringing back these lists with 40 and 70 and 500 names and I brought back one, mine. Then the Associate Director decided he was gonna chastise me and he says, "O.K., I got something I want you to do. I want you to transfer these names to file cards." I said, "Naw, man. That's secretarial work and that ain't my job." "Well, that's what I want you to do." So I said, Groovy, and I took the cards and a piece of paper and wrote my letter of resignation and gave him the cards and the letter. The Director called me in and asked me was I sure this was what I wanted to do. I told him that I wasn't about to sit there and write names on cards. He said, "That's your decision." And I said, "Yeah, that's my decision." And I split.

8 Ever since Ed and I have been active in the Movement we've always carried our guns. I've always had the utmost confidence in me and the gun. Give me a gun before you even give me somebody to work with. A gun won't fail you. People will. I found that out early. I never went on any large demonstrations 'cause I knew that if somebody hit me I just wasn't going to stand there and take no beating. I've been tear-gassed, but they've never put dogs on me or nothing like that. The whole thing is that if you can woof and woof hard enough and long enough and be willing to back it up, few people will push you. I've been in a lot of police stations and I've never been beaten. I've never been hit in a police station 'cause I make it very clear that if you get me, I'm gonna get me somebody. And the cops don't know which one of 'em it's going to be. I tell 'em, "I'm gonna just work on one muthafucka. I don't care about the rest of y'all. I know y'all gonna get to me sooner or later, but I'm gonna get me one, you can believe that." Ain't no fool called my bluff yet. And if they ever do, I know I can back it up.

Everybody's able to defend themselves, but few are willing. You got to be able and willing. That's the whole concept. All my life that's what's been preserving me. And I don't think there's any need for me to change. Nonviolence might have been tactically correct at one time in order to get some sympathy for the Movement, but for me as an individual, it just never worked. And I didn't try to convince myself that it would work.

When I was in school and I'd be coming off the block late

at night, white folks always used to try messing with any blood they saw by pointing their little peashooters out the window and simple shit like that. This one night, I was making it on in and two jive muthafucking white dudes passed by in a black '50 Ford and gave me the finger. Now I realize that I could've let it pass and just shrugged it off, but I figured that the dudes didn't have no right to do that. So I screamed at 'em: "Fuck your mammy!" They turned around and came back. It was two of them and just me, so they must've figured I was gonna run. I ran. Sho' did. Ran and picked up a beer bottle, broke the bottom off and started running toward 'em. Well, they got on the other side of the intersection and were screaming, "We see that bottle you got! We see it!" I was steady woofing at them muthafuckas. All the time, though, I was hoping that some of my boys would just happen to be coming through. But the crackers wouldn't come across the street where I was. They just stood over there and hollered. This old cracker was passing by and he asked 'em what was wrong. They said I started some shit with 'em. Well, this old white dude convinced 'em that they should go ahead and leave me alone, 'cause there wasn't no sense in them crossing the street to where I was and getting cut up. So they split. It was then that I decided to start carrying a gun. I figured that if the police could carry a gun to police my community, then I should carry one to police them and the other uppity crackers. The first gun I owned I stole from a sporting store when I was fourteen.

I've been around guns all my life, so it's never been a big thing with me. My old man hunts, and you talk about a dude who can shoot. That man could hit a gnat in the navel from 400 yards with a B.B. gun. I ain't lying. He took me and Ed hunting once. I must have been about twelve or thirteen. It was cold! Jim, it was cold! I ain't never seen it so cold. It was cold as polar bear shit. He'd bought us some rubber boots, but he didn't really hip us as to what to put on in those boots, so I just put on a pair of nylon socks and no shoes or nothing. And that cat took us out in the woods about ten or eleven o'clock and walked us till about three in the morning. We carried the gun and the game and we never shot the whole night. He'd shoot and put it in the bag and we'd have to carry it around. So we didn't go hunting with him no more. I used to hunt a lot by myself. But my old man! He can shoot! If you ain't three miles away, don't fuck with him. Get out of range of the gun, 'cause if he can see you, he can hit you.

To my knowledge, though, my ol' man never used a gun against anybody. He used to box, so he didn't need to pull a gun. He's a big ol' dude. About 230 pounds and he stands about six foot one. My old man can pick up a 500-pound oil barrel and walk away with it. He don't have to worry about shooting nobody. But it seemed to me that my old man was always more ready to whip me than the folks who oughta be whipped. Like the first time I got arrested. I was fifteen or sixteen at the time. Me and my man Freddie Williams were coming home from school and I was carrying my book bag. Naturally, there weren't any books in the bag. Just my gun. So Freddie had to stop in this store downtown and I went in with him. It was around Christmas time. Well, you know how white folks watch niggers when they go in stores. I wasn't hanging around the merchandise or nothing, but when I walked out, this cracker store detective walks up to me and says, "Lemme see what you got in that bag." I said, "What you mean, let you see?" Cause I knew I had my shit in the bag and I wasn't for letting the muthafucka see it. Well, he called a cop over and pulled his gun, so I said, "Well, solid." The cop looked in the bag, and naturally he saw what I had inside. He called the station and they took me in and booked me. Well, my ol' man came down, bitching and woofing and raising hell. But it was all directed at me. I told him, "You don't have to get me out." He got me out, but he kept on bitching at me. I said, "Dig, I didn't get out just to hear all this shit." But he's moaning about how it's Christmas time and he used all the money to get me out on bond. That was all he could think of.

Folks have always had difficulty trying to deal with the fact that I carry a gun. Even people in SNCC. The first time I got busted in Alabama, it was on a concealed weapon charge, and people in the Atlanta SNCC office wanted to know why I had a gun. This was in 1966 when SNCC was talking Black Power. They debated over whether or not to get me out of jail and they didn't. Ed put up my bond. That was some shaky muthafucking shit. But I made it very clear to them. Yeah, I would give up my .38 when they gave me a laser gun. If *you're* gonna woof at the muthafucka, then I'm gon' carry some shit to back up the woof. They could put me out of the organization, but they weren't taking my gun. I knew that bubble gum and rocks ain't no good against that other shit. The only thing "the man's" going to respect is that .45 or .38 you got. That's what it all boils down to.

A lot of people, though, are afraid to defend their own lives. They're afraid to take a chance for their own liberation. But there's no other way to be free unless you put your life on the line. A lot of people are mad at me now, because they say that me and Carmichael and other dudes who've been out there talking are only setting the stage for the extermination of Black people. Well, if 30 million people have to go to free the people in Vietnam and Africa, fuck it. We've been living too long anyway. Only people who've never lived fear death. If you've lived, you know that death is part of the process. A lot of people say that it's regrettable that Malcolm got killed. But Malcolm was not an individual. His life didn't belong to him. No revolutionary can claim his life for himself. The life of the revolutionary belongs to the struggle. Malcolm, like Che, is not dead, because he was totally committed to the struggle. The only people who should make any kind of statement of regret over Malcolm's death are Malcolm's family. Death is the price of revolution. Malcolm assumed that responsibility and he knew what role he was playing. The shame is that the people who're going around screaming Malcolm now wouldn't listen to Malcolm when he was living.

Malcolm was the first Black leader to come out and tell Black people that they had a right to defend their own lives. Of course, it was negroes who needed to hear that, not Blacks. The brother on the block carried a knife in his diaper. He knew where it was at. America doesn't rule the world with love. It rules with guns, tanks, missiles, bombs, the Army, Air Force, Navy and the Marines. When america fights a nonviolent war, I'll become nonviolent. But I ain't gon' hold my breath waiting for that day to come around. People want to say that I preach violence. I preach a response to violence. Meet violence with violence. If you're minding your business and someone starts fucking with you, he's being violent, because he's infringing on your human rights. It's your responsibility to jump back at the muthafucka and make him back down or fight. If you don't, he knows that you're scared and that he can control you and that's your ass.

In '66 and '67 when I was working in Greene County, Alabama, for SNCC, I was always having confrontations with honkies who thought I shouldn't be there organizing Black people or didn't like the way I carried myself. I knew that it was my job and my responsibility to work for the liberation of my people and anybody who tried to stop me might get killed.

From the first day I got to Greene County, the honkies tried to run me out. I was driving down to see Mr. Gilmore, this negro cat that was the candidate for sheriff on the Freedom ballot. I was doing about 70 or 80 and there were these honkies picketing this electrical work company. I shot through there and honkies screamed something at me. I threw on the brakes and backed up. Wasn't nobody in the car but me and George Greene and George don't take no shit off white folks, either. And, of course, I had my action with me, a .38. I backed up and said, "What'd you say?" This honky said, "I said don't be coming through here that fast. Don't you see those men over there?" They were over on the other side of the road. I said, "What you the police or something?" "Naw, I just—I say don't be coming through here that fast." I just drove off. I went on down to Mr. Gilmore's. He wasn't at home, so I turned around and went back through there, doing 80 again. I saw the honky and another cracker run and get in his car, but they couldn't catch me. So I turned off to the side of the road and waited for them to pull in behind me. I jumped out and I had my gun with me. And even though he saw my gun, he was going to try and scare me. So I said, "What you want? You trying to catch me?" "I told you not to go through there again," he said. I said, "Who in the fuck are you? If you ain't the police, you ain't got a damned thing to say to me." I was woofing at the chump and George Greene got out the other side of the car. This other cracker, though, who had acted the fool and jumped in the car wasn't saying nothing. He just sat there trembling and smiling.

So the honky says, "You just come through there like that one more time!" I told him, "You better get the fuck from

86

around me. That's what you'd better do, boy." And that's what he did. This kind of thing happens all the time. White folks feel that they just got to chastise Black people. If it had been a white boy, he wouldn't have jumped in his car and gone chasing him. So, I just had to put him in his place.

Just before I left Alabama, I pulled my gun on a sheriff and two deputies. I had gone to see this girl that I'd met in Selma. She was working with the Department of Labor. She traveled in an integrated team and had this white girl with her. They were going to some place called Jackson, Alabama, which is 50 miles from Mobile. I went down to spend a couple of days with her when this white girl was going to New Orleans or somewhere. The white folks in town were already suspicious, 'cause they didn't like the two of them living and working together. I guess the hotel must've had the line tapped, 'cause they knew I was coming. They were trying to lay a trap, as I soon found out, so they would have an excuse to get the two chicks out of the area.

Well, I drove into town carrying my riot gun. Had me a riot gun, a .12 gauge that would shoot seven times and chunk bricks for a half hour. You were supposed to plug it. But I wasn't about to.

I went down there and I had brought some rum with me, so we were copping some t.v. and were gon' drink some rum and just party. All of a sudden I heard a key turn in the door. The sister had put the chain on, so when they pushed it, the chain held the door. I looked out the door and saw all these crackers out there. My first reaction was, what the fuck is going on? I jumped up and got my gun.

They had on ordinary clothes and they looked like regular ol' crackers. Then I dug that they had guns and I realized that I was standing right in front of them. So I moved to the side of the door. One of 'em says, "I'm the sheriff." I said, "You got to do better than that." So he put his little badge through the door. "O.K. What you want?" He said, "Open the door." I said, "She-e-it." But the chick kept saying "Open the door, open the door." So I decided to let them in 'cause I had the drop on 'em.

So I closed the door and took the chain off and let them in. I had the gun on 'em, so if they moved, I moved. The sheriff had a camera in his hand and the other cracker had his pistol. I had the drop on 'em and the muthafucka with the pistol eased it down when he saw that. So I'm standing there talkin' to 'em and another pig eased through the door and put a .38 dead to my head. "All right. Drop that muthafucka." That gun was up against my head so hard I could feel the bullet in the chamber. So I figured, Well, solid. That's the way the deal goes down sometimes. "You got me," I said, and I put my shit down. Then he told me I was under arrest.

Well, you know me. By now this was just routine so I said, "Under arrest! For what?" Hell, I could think of forty charges myself. I knew damned well they wasn't gon' let a nigger get the drop on the sheriff and then let him go, but you got to stay on the offensive all the time. "What you mean I'm under arrest? For what, goddammit?" I was woofing like a champ. Well, the muthafucka said I was under arrest for fornication and a violation of prohibition. It was a dry county and we were drinking rum. Then he looked at the riot gun and said, "Also, a violation of the Federal Firearms Act. This gun is too short." I said, "Naw, it ain't too short!" But they arrested me and the sister. It was her first time going to jail and it really upset her. Her first course in being a sho-nuf nigger. I was impressed at the way she maintained herself and I wondered how many other sisters in situations similar to ours would be as together as she was. (The test will come.)

They took us to the jail, which was about 17 miles away.

When we got there I found out that they knew who I was, who I worked for and what time I'd left Selma. The camera had been brought over to take pictures, for evidence. They thought we were screwing and they were going to take pictures for the trial, or for their wives—one of the two. Fornication (screwing) is against the law. If they really tried to enforce that law, there'd be a revolution tomorrow. But to even have laws like that shows how messed up white people are. This country is probably the only country in the world with a law against screwing.

The charges against the sister were eventually dropped. The government provided her defense, and me, well, I had to defend myself. This was not my first time having to do this, and, although I have never won a case, I was ready. My defense was sound, too sound. After the conviction, the judge said since I knew so much about law, he was going to give me some time to study. The only way I finally got out of that was that my main man, Howard Moore, SNCC attorney in Atlanta, came and bought me for $200 and brought me back to outside slavery.

9 SNCC, as an organization, had come into Alabama after the summer of 1964, following the Mississippi challenge. People were sent in to organize Black voters. I went to work in the state in the fall of '66. The election was coming up, and Carmichael who was Chairman then had appointed Stanley Wise to coordinate it. We had candidates running in Lowndes County, Dallas County, and potentially, Greene County, where I was working. However, in Greene County we would have to fight just to get the candidates on the ballot. I was director of the Greene County Project. George Greene was the first cat to come over. Marc Lewis, who later proved to be one of the hardest workers, came next. Eric Jones, my roommate from Washington D.C., decided to take a year off from school to come and work. That was staff for a good while. Later, a cat named Snake came over from Mississippi.

At first, we just spent our time going to meetings and getting to know the people, just basic organizing. As it got closer to election time, we found out that the power structure didn't have any intention of putting the Black candidates' names on the ballot. So we began to talk about a "Freedom Election," which would create a parallel government; Black people are 87% of the country. We were trying to get people to see that people are the real government. Establish your own government in opposition to this corrupt government and if it calls for a confrontation, be prepared for that. Then let the federal government decide whose government is legitimate. (We talked about the federal government coming into it just to get people to move in the direction of local self-government. I knew, however, which side the federal government would take.) People began to dig the idea. So I drafted a letter to Johnson, the Attorney General, the Governor and the Attorney General of Alabama. And I told them that we, the Black Panther Party, were gonna hold freedom elections and boycott the regular election, because our candidates' names would not appear on the ballot.

It was surprising what started to develop then. The old-line negro leadership, the ministers, and even Mr. Gilmore, didn't want to be labelled the Black Panther Party. Gilmore had some experience working with SCLC and he was still in that integration bag and he liked to take trips up north to talk to white folks and shit like that. But we were working with the poor people out in the community and were developing a base. We were gonna hold our own election and let the people decide who they wanted.

One day, a week before the election, George Greene and I went downtown. George was going to buy an axe handle. While we were there they accused us of trying to steal a gun and arrested us for grand larceny. Hell, I had an arsenal already. What I need to steal a gun for? But it was just a way to get us out of action until after the election. They held us on $1,000 bond.

While we were in jail, we saw in the newspapers that they had postponed the election as a result of the pressure that we had mounted in the community. They were claiming that the Freedom candidates had been nominated illegally, although Alabama has a law which says that they can be nominated by mass meeting. Getting the elections postponed was a victory for us.

We were bailed out on the 7th of November. Elections were scheduled for the 8th, but since they had been postponed, we went over to Lowndes County. We set up defense positions there for election night, 'cause we knew that the honkies were preparing some shit. They were pretty pissed off, not only about niggers being on the ballot, but niggers voting. So everybody was armed. White folks jumped on a brother over in Fort Deposit. Niggers didn't do nothing, so I left. I thought that we should at least jack up 10 or 12 crackers.

When we got back to Greene County, we found out that George Wallace said his wife had won every county but one —Greene County. No greater tribute could have been paid to our work than that. Wallace said that his wife lost Greene County because of the Black Power niggers over there.

After the elections, Carmichael asked me to take over the state of Alabama, to become state project director. It was a nice title, but I was still starving. Up in Greene County, we used to starve like dogs. The house we lived in didn't have running water and it had newspapers on the walls and the floors. Folks in the community would feed you if they respected your work, and they fed us a lot even though they were starving too. We couldn't expect them to feed us all of the time, so I'd go down to the P&B and liberate food.

The most gratifying and rewarding experiences in this field of work come from the relationship that is developed between the people you work with and for. In Alabama there was one man who earned the respect of all the staff. Strong individuals are not uncommon in the struggle. This man, however, became an image that inspired in us a new dimension of Black peoplehood. Here was a man who placed the good of people before personal interest and safety. His involvement in the struggle was complete. And next to his family of ten children, this struggle was his greatest concern. He called his friends, "fellow," and because this was his favorite word most of his friends called him the same. I called him Mr. Jackson, Mr. Matthew Jackson, because of the respect I had for him. Mr. Jackson had become a legend in his own time. He was thought of by staff as being the baddest man in Alabama. Ralph Featherstone could talk about experiences that he and Mr. Jackson had with crackers that would make us wonder if Featherstone was lying. But knowing Mr. Jackson, we assumed them to be true. However, Mr. Jackson represented much more than just a bad man; to us he was a complete individual. His education had come as a result of living.

Although he was not unusually large physically, one could sense by his very presence his enormous strength both spiritually and physically. And though he was fighting man's endless war with age, it appeared that he had won more battles than he had lost. We all knew that this was a good man to have on our side. Mr. Jackson would always say, "Fellow, I can't take it but so far, then it's up to you, I done fought my best fight." I would always tell him, "Man, wait till you get my age, you don't know what trouble is." And he would smile and say, "Fellow, you all right." Mr. Jackson could work until people who were just looking at him began to sweat. I would go in the field in the early morning with him and leave at noon to go out in the county, and when I came back around six he would still be working. And then he would come to meeting later that night.

Once SNCC assigned people to a county, it was up to them to find places to live and food to eat. It was because of Mr. Jackson that those who went to Lowndes didn't have much trouble in doing either. Anything SNCC people needed that was around, was shared with them. Mr. Jackson gave all of his children to the Movement. His sons James, Leon and Johnnie all joined staff of the national organization of SNCC. Bob Mants, who was SNCC's top organizer and backbone of the Lowndes County Movement, was responsible for their political education. People throughout the county even now talk about some of the things Bob and the Jackson sons did.

Mr. Jackson was especially fond of children and he had the greatest capacity to love them of any man I can remember. He would go to any length to spoil them and would dismiss any criticism with a slight gesture of his hand. He was politician, soldier and conscience of the Lowndes County Movement. Danny Brown, one of SNCC's Alabama staff members, has said that next to himself, Mr. Jackson is the most complete revolutionary living. We all learned a lot from this man.

In February a brother named Buttercup was killed by a white cop in Autaugua County. This county is famous for two things: Pratt Mountain, which is the state meeting place for the Ku Klux Klan and Ladybird's plantation. I was invited over from Selma (which is where our state office is located) by some people who lived in Prattville, the city where Buttercup was killed. I had to travel by myself 'cause we didn't have enough staff and I couldn't take people from other projects. I went over and organized a political organization and a defensive organization. They were strong because there were a lot of young brothers in them. One night the people in Prattville wanted to march down to see the mayor and the sheriff. I knew it wouldn't do any good, but I didn't want to stop that kind of action. It was a positive step. So I said, "Okay, we'll go see the sheriff and the mayor." When we got downtown there were only about three or four crackers standing around. They started getting nasty with the Black folks and the bloods were just taking it. So, I started screaming on the crackers. You've got to implant in people's minds that you don't take no shit, that you're as equal as any human. So, I started signifying and the people were laughing and appreciating it. I said, "Where's the sheriff? He's scared to come out here and talk to us?" So the sheriff came out and said, "I'll talk to anybody who lives in this county. The rest of y'all got to get out." That meant me and Jake, a SNCC brother who was working with me at the time, and a white chick who was a reporter for the *Southern Courier*. She was a pain in the ass. So me and Jake went on out. Well, the word had gotten out that Black folks were downtown. While we were standing outside, the crackers started gathering around and this stupid, jive reporter chick came looking up in our faces asking stupid questions. Each time she'd get next to Jake he would move over to my other side, keeping me between him and the bitch. Finally I told her to get away from us and that we had nothing to say. So we decided to sit in the car. Then she came over to the car talking about can she get in the car. I said, "You better get away from this car."

The crackers were really coming out in force now. This one cracker ran across the street and made a telephone call and then soon after someone drove up and gave him a pistol. Some of 'em had pistols sticking out of their belts. Jake started saying, "Let's go, man. Let's get the fuck out of here." I told him, "No, we can't leave the people like that. We brought them down here and we got to wait for 'em." The mayor and sheriff were really setting the people up because they were letting the white local forces gather.

A state trooper car pulled up and Jake said, "Oh, Lawd, I know the shit's gonna start now. They gon' start some shit." He wasn't lying about that. These muthafuckas were famous for starting shit. They had on black leather jackets and they pulled up where the crackers were standing. The crackers jumped up on the trooper's car letting us know that these were their boys. Then another trooper car pulled up and Jake says, "Lawd man, let's go." I guessed we both were scared, but I just wasn't for leaving our people in the sheriff's office, 'cause I didn't know what was gonna break when they came out. I was hoping they would hurry up and come out before the crowd got too big.

Finally they came out, and you've never seen anything so

beautiful. Those young brothers came out there woofing, diddy-bopping and raising hell. They had won their confrontation. They had met "the man" and found out that when you stop being controlled by fear, then the people you were once afraid of are afraid of you.

10 In May of 1967 I was elected Chairman of SNCC. It was not a position which I sought, but people seemed to feel that I would be a good one to articulate the positions of the organization. Even though the press began projecting me as a "Black Power leader" and all that kind of mess, I knew that it didn't matter what position a dude had, it didn't mean he was a leader, even if he had the title of Chairman or President. The leader might be a dude in the organization who ain't got no title, no office. When I was head of SNCC, that's all I was. I was not a leader of Black people. I had a public platform because I was Chairman of SNCC and therefore what I said got heard by a lot of people. But I don't think I can articulate the sentiments of Black folks any better than the brothers and sisters did in Detroit. I'm just in a position where maybe I can explain what the brother is talking about, because there're a lot of negroes who don't understand. That does not mean leadership.

It was obvious when I became Chairman that I was in for trouble. For a year, "the man" had let Carmichael travel around the country talking about Black Power and "the man" realized that he had made a serious mistake. He recognized too late that Black people, like the Vietnamese people, were escalating their war of liberation. So it was clear to me that if Black people began to respond by accepting a revolutionary analysis, "the man" was going to try and silence me. But if you're serious you don't worry about things like that. You do your job and you're either carried off the battlefield or you walk off victorious.

The first move that the government made against me came in the last week of July, '67, when I went to speak in Cambridge, Maryland. I almost missed going to Cambridge. Gloria Dandridge, who was Gloria Richardson when she led the Cambridge Movement, set up a speaking engagement for me down there. I'd been to Cambridge when she was leading the Movement there, so I was familiar with what had been happening.

I was scheduled to speak at 7:30 at night, but I missed the bus. So I had to fly to Baltimore and then take another chartered flight. I got to Cambridge about an hour late and the people were still waiting. Well, the Black community was full of negro cops. And there were white cops and National Guardsmen on Race Street. That's the street which divides the Black community from the white. They were stationed in front of all the stores.

I spoke and afterwards I went up to the local office of the Movement. There wasn't anything going on. People were just standing around talking, both in the office and out on the street and everything was cool. There was this young sister who wanted us to walk her home because she was afraid. She lived near Race Street and she was afraid of all those white cops that were stationed down there. So I was walking down the street with her and I noticed that everybody who was around was walking with us. They were just tagging along behind us, which ain't too cool a thing to do. We got about halfway down the street and somebody opened fire from some bushes which were behind me. So people began to scatter. I got shot—I was hit in the head with some of the shotgun pellets. I dove on the ground and rolled over up against this wooden fence. There were three of us trapped out there—a girl, another brother and myself. The cops who were doing the shooting just kept shooting. For about five minutes they sustained their fire and they were steadily

100

knocking splinters out of that fence. And you talk about getting low. The Vietcong ain't had nothing on me about getting low. The brother was getting kind of nervous and wanted to try and get out of there. I figured the safest thing to do was to stay low because I didn't know whether there were other cops around just waiting for us to try and make a run for it. But he wanted to get on out and he told me to get up and let him by. I told him that I wasn't about to get up. So he crawled around me and went about 15 yards and he found a gate that was open. He yelled back and told us so I crawled on down there. The girl was too scared to move. Just as I got to the gate, he struck a match to light a cigarette. "Put that match out!" I told him but by then the police had seen the match and opened fire on us. By that time, though, I was through the gate.

We got away and I went to somebody's house to try and get myself a little first aid. I was still bleeding. The people stopped the bleeding and got me to a doctor's office. He gave me some kind of shot, which made me dizzy. By this time the brothers had heard what had happened and they were mad and had gone home to get their pieces.

I went back out in the streets to see what was going on. The brothers were out and they were hiding on both sides of the street so that if any crackers came down through there, they had them in a cross fire. The only thing wrong was that the brothers would've ended up shooting each other, because they had their cross fire laid out wrong. So I told 'em. I left after that.

The next day, while in Washington, D.C., I heard that there was a 13-state federal warrant out for my arrest. So I called William Kunstler, SNCC's New York attorney and he told me that the FBI had contacted him and wanted to work out some way for me to surrender. I said, "Surrender!! She - e - it." Kunstler decided that I should come to New

York and surrender there. Well, I wasn't in favor of surrendering. Let the muthafuckas come and get me. However, I knew this was not the time, so I said, O.K., and told him that I'd come up the next day. The whole thing was set up for the following noon.

The next day I went to National Airport to catch the plane to New York and surrender. When I left the house that morning I saw this dude standing outside and I knew he was "the man." When I got to the airport, I thought the FBI was having a convention, there were so many of them. I was dressed in my dungarees so it was obvious that I wasn't trying to sneak out of town. Wasn't no way in the world I could disguise myself and I didn't see no point in trying to hide. I hadn't done a damned thing but exercise my right to "Free Speech."

I went on down and got a shuttle pass and the airport police came up to me. "Are you Rap Brown?" I said, "Yeah." "Would you come with us?" I said, "For what?" "There's a warrant out for your arrest." I said, "I know it. I'm going to New York to surrender to the Federal Bureau of Faggots. That's where I'm on my way to now." They said, "Well, we have to notify the authorities." I said, "Good. Call the FBI because the agreement was made with them." Well, they called the muthafuckas and the pigs denied it so they came back with some more pigs. I called Kunstler and explained to him what had happened. It was obvious to me by that time that I had been the victim of a setup. They'd never intended to let me get to New York. They could've arrested me there in Washington because they knew where I was staying. But they wanted to make it appear as if I was trying to run away.

I was arrested and taken to Alexandria, Virginia, and was in the custody of the Virginia authorities. They put me in jail and sent this negro FBI agent to interrogate me. I blew

102

that bootlicker's mind. I told him, "Now, you know why they sent you in here. If I was Bobby Baker, you wouldn't be here. You wouldn't be nowhere around here. Only reason they sent you in here is 'cause they think I'm gon' talk to you because you're cullard." I laughed at him. "I know you got a little tape recorder on you." He come asking me what I thought of Mao. I told him, "You raised the subject, you talk about it. Otherwise let's talk about these crackers." I said, "Did you know that Hoover is a faggot—your boss?" I asked him, "Did he ever hit on you?" So he got scared and left.

Well, they took me down to be arraigned. By this time my lawyer had come down from New York. The deal was that the federal government would drop the charges about me being a fugitive, but Virginia would re-arrest me to be held for extradition to Maryland.

When the federal government released me, I was on federal property and I decided to stay because the Virginia authorities couldn't arrest me as long at I was on federal property. (So the story goes.) Well, the federal government ejected me from the building. When I got out on the steps, a lot of Black folks had come over from Washington, D.C. I told them to bring me some lumber. They could have my 40 acres and a mule, I was setting up camp right there on the steps. Well, that's when a little shoving contest began. The federal marshalls tried to shove me off the steps and I shoved them and they shoved me and eventually they shoved me on out into the street where I was arrested by the Virginia cops. They also arrested my man, Donald Brown, who was then a student at Howard. I guess they didn't want anything brown in their white town.

They put me in the city jail in Alexandria and when the Black community got the word they came down to the jail. I heard a lot of noise and I didn't find out until later that they had come down there and were willing to break me

103

out. And who stopped them? The militants! The so-called revolutionaries! "Don't you see all them guns?" Well, the people saw all the guns. If they could've broken in there and gotten me out, I was for leaving with 'em. But the militants were out there stopping the revolutionary process. That showed me where the militants were at. If the revolution is abortive, it'll be because of them. They're the people who talk the most and when it comes time for action, they won't shut up. They gon' stop the people.

Half of the Black "militants" ain't nothing but a bunch of potheads, bootleg preachers and coffeehouse intellectuals. They are caught up in that whole identity thing. They just discovered that they were Black, because they were working so hard all their lives to be white. They're further away from being revolutionaries than the poor people who are not militantly political. But the coffeehouse intellectual, the Black militant, thinks he's political because he reads Fanon. Books don't make revolutionaries. I contend that the Black people who burned down Watts and Detroit don't have to read. These cats have lived more than the intellectual has read. So they are political by having learned from their existence. Oppression made these cats political. The militants spend all their time trying to program white people into giving them some money. "The man" has created a new type of Tom. They are willing to be anything, as long as they can be Black first. Black capitalists, Black imperialists, Black oppressors—anything, so long as it's Black first.

While I was in jail in Alexandria, I wrote what was to become a series of Letters from Jail. I didn't plan it like that but that's how it's been working out. I feel when I'm in jail that the people should understand very clearly that the reason I'm in jail is because my crime is political, because I've spoken out against injustices. When I was arrested after Cambridge, the press tried to portray me as some kind of danger-

ous outlaw. So in my Letter from Jail, I raised the question:
Who Are the Real Outlaws?

Brothers and Sisters,

*White people are saying that the uprisings of our
people in almost 100 american cities, "must be a conspiracy."* Where is the real conspiracy? *Black people
across this country have known that the real conspiracy
in this country is to run us out, keep us down or kill us,
if we can't act like the honky wants us to act.*

*We're fighting for our survival and for this we are
called criminals, outlaws and murderers.* Who are the
real criminals? *Who stole us from Africa? Who has been
stealing our labor these past 400 years to build this
country?* Who are the real murderers? *Why don't they
call the police who gun us down in the streets every
day, all year 'round . . . why don't they call them murderers?*

*Why don't they call Lyndon Johnson a murderer and
an outlaw? He fights an illegal war with our brothers
and our sons. He sends them to fight against other
people of color who are also fighting for their freedom.*

Who are the real outlaws in this country? *They say I
am an outlaw. I am charged with inciting Black people
to "riot." It is against the "law" to riot. But did you
or I have any say in passing this law? Do we have
much of a say in any of the laws passed in this country?
I consider myself neither morally nor legally bound to
obey laws which were made by a group of white "lawmakers" who did not let my people be represented in
making those laws.*

*That government which makes laws that you and I
are supposed to obey, without letting us be a part of
that government . . . is an illegal government. The men*

who pass those laws are outlaws; the police who enforce those laws are outlaws and murderers.

It should be understandable that we, as Black people, should adopt the attitude that we are neither morally nor legally bound to obey laws which were not made with our consent and which seek to keep us "in our place." Nor can we be expected to have confidence in the white man's courts which interpret and enforce those laws. The white man makes all the laws, he drags us before his courts, he accuses us, and he sits in judgment over us.

White america should not fool itself into believing that if it comes down harder on us that that will keep us from doing what we believe is right. History has shown that when a man's consciousness is aroused, when a man really believes what he is doing, threats of jail and death cannot turn that man back. The threat of jail or death will not turn me nor others like me from the path we have taken.

We stand on the eve of a Black revolution. These rebellions are but a dress rehearsal for real revolution. For to men, freedom in their own land is the pinnacle of their ambitions, and nothing can turn men aside who have conviction and a strong sense of freedom.

More powerful than my fear of what could happen to me in prison is my hatred for what happens to my people in those outside prisons called the Black ghettoes of this country. I hate the practice of race discrimination, and in my hatred I am supported by the fact that the overwhelming majority of mankind hates it equally. There is nothing any court can do to me that will change that hatred in me; it can only be changed by the removal of the racism and inhumanity which exist in this country.

106

A society which can mount a huge military action against a Black youth who breaks a window, and at the same time plead that it is powerless to protect Black youths who are being murdered each year because they seek to make democracy in america a reality, is a sick, criminal and insane society. They talk about violence in the country's streets! Each time a Black church is bombed or burned, that is violence in our streets! Where are the troops?

Each time a Black body is found in the swamps of Mississippi or Alabama, that is violence in our land! Where are those murderers?

Each time Black human rights workers are refused protection by the government, that is anarchy!

Each time a police officer shoots and kills a Black teenager, that is urban crime! Where is the national leader who will go on t.v. and condemn police crime?

Black people see america for what it is. It is clear now that white america cannot condemn itself, cannot see the reality of its crimes against mankind. We see america for what it is: the Fourth Reich . . . and we recognize our course of action.

The repeated attempts that the government has made to silence me represent just one level of genocide that is practiced by america. This genocide can be seen on many different levels. It can be seen actively in Vietnam where 45 percent of the frontline casualties are Black. That's no accident. Another level of genocide can be seen operating in the South, where many Black people live on a starvation level. Over 500 Black people die in Alabama each year for lack of proper food and nourishment. This is happening in a country that sends people to the moon. Yet another level of genocide can be seen in the courts. Any Black man across america who

107

faces a white judge or who faces any court procedure can expect the maximum fine and the maximum sentence. Muhammad Ali, LeRoi Jones, Huey Newton, Ed Oquenda, myself, and thousands of Black men and women across the country have been thrown into prison because we have stood up and challenged the system. Some of the best minds in the Black community are in jail and that's genocide. The most obvious example of genocide is in the concentration camps that america has prepared for Black people. This came about as a result of the McCarran Act of 1950, a law which establishes concentration camps. There is a part, Title II, which suspends the right of due process. That means that there goes the dissolution of all machinery whereby you would be entitled to see a lawyer or go to court. You're arrested and taken off to the camp, without having had an opportunity to state your side of the case. Not that the presentation of your case matters.

At the present time, america still lets us use her "legal" machinery and, through legal maneuvers, my attorney was able to get me freed. But this was only after the court set ridiculously high bail. This is nothing short of ransom. I anticipate one day, however, that I will be arrested and there will be no legal procedure any lawyer will be able to use to secure my release. In fact, the first question will not be, Let's get Rap out of jail. It'll be, Where is Rap?

11

From the time of my release until my next arrest in September, I was followed 24 hours a day by negro pigs. I thought so little of the muthafuckas that I would come out of the house in the morning and jump into their car and tell 'em to take me wherever I was going. I would talk to the chumps and try to make 'em see that when "the man" decided to move against Black people he would move against them first. They weren't exempt because they were cops. In fact, they were more of a threat. No Black man is trusted. But the chumps couldn't see it. I told 'em about the negro cop in Newark who went to the station to report for duty when the Newark rebellion broke out. The white pigs saw him come walking into the stationhouse and they kicked his ass. All the while he was yelling, "I'm a cop! I'm a cop!" All the white cops saw was a nigger and they kicked his Black ass until somebody white recognized the chump. And even then I bet them white cops didn't apologize. But the negro didn't have no better sense than to get up and put a sheepish grin on his face and go put on his uniform. Negroes like that deserve to get their asses kicked.

My second arrest came about through a law that I know the government had to put 200 cats to work to even find, it was so old. I'd bought a rifle, which was not illegal at that time, and it was a sweet mama-jammer, too. I purchased it the same day that I was due to go to Baton Rouge to see my folks, so I carried it with me. When I got on the plane, I informed the stewardess what I had in the plastic bag I was carrying and asked her to hold it for me. There was never any secret about what I was carrying. I spent a couple of days in Baton Rouge and then went on back to New York. The night I arrived in New York I was supposed to have continued on to Cincinnati for a speaking engagement the next day. Instead, I stayed in New York with a friend, Allen Bailey (better known as the Prime Minister of Harlem). Someone came into the house around 2 A.M. and said that the neighborhood was filled with cops. During this time I was under 24-hour surveillance anyway. So, cops weren't unusual. But he said that there were 20 or 30 out there. So I went to the door to see and while standing there these two bootlicking, ass-kissing negro cops of the N.Y.P.D., who were assigned to follow me, called me out to the curb. At this time about 20 white pigs converged on me. They told me that they were from the Alcohol and Tobacco Division and that I was under arrest. Knowing that I don't drink or smoke, I said, "Man, you must have the wrong dude. I don't indulge!" They arrested me for transporting a rifle across state lines while under federal indictment. I've heard of some bullshit laws, but that is about number one. I didn't even know I was under indictment. The only thing hanging over my head was extradition hearings in Virginia. But seeing as how I was outnumbered by about twenty to one, I decided that I wasn't going to dispute the matter. I also decided that the day would come when odds didn't matter.

I was jailed in New York and held on $25,000 bond. Kunstler eventually got that reduced to $15,000 which SNCC had to raise in cash. No bondsman would handle the case. This was simply a tactic to make it more difficult for me to get out of jail. By the time I did get out of jail, however, "the man" had decided that I was going to be grounded for a while. I was sent from New York to New Orleans, where the judge said that when I went back to New York I was not to travel anywhere outside the Southern District of New York which meant that I couldn't even go to Queens or Brooklyn. I said, Damn! I'm gon' have to get the cracker's O.K. to go to the bathroom. The judge in Virginia decided that he wanted a piece of me, too, and he said that I couldn't travel anywhere in the country without getting his approval.

It was very clear that I was, in effect, under house arrest. So I said, Solid. Whatever they do to me is not going to stop the revolution. Anybody who is projected as a leader generally impedes the revolution anyway. Whether I was out there or not, I knew that the brothers were going to take care of business. A revolution doesn't depend on one person. In actuality, the revolutionary is an unknown person. He's the brother who's taking care of business, the one who's getting his head together, the one who's in the street, the one who dies in the rebellions. Like in Vietnam, he's the one who is known only to his cell leader, or his commander. He's the cat whose name never appears in history books. It ain't the dude with the natural. I'd rather see a cat with a processed head and a natural mind than a natural head and a processed mind. It ain't what's on your head; it's what's in it. You see negroes with naturals on their heads and nothing on their minds. Revolutionaries are not determined by physical characteristics. Some of the most revolutionary people in Vietnam are women, but we got muthafuckas here running around talking about let the men do it all.

So it didn't bother me that I was going to be grounded for a while. The struggle was going to go on.

In February, 1968, Kunstler went out to California and I had to go out to consult with him about one of the cases. I figured that I didn't need the court's permission to go as I could travel anywhere to consult with my attorney. While I was in California I checked out the scene and the brothers asked me to speak at a couple of meetings, which I did. I was out there for two days and then split on back to New York.

The morning after I got back, eight federal marshals knocked on my door. First they'd called my house to make sure I was there. When I picked up the phone this voice said he had the wrong number. Well, I figured who it was, but I didn't know what their next move was going to be. A few minutes after that, here comes these eight federal marshalls in front of my door with their guns drawn.

I looked through the peephole in the door and saw all these honkies with their pistols and I said, "Yeah, What'cha want?" They said, "Open the door." I said, "Now come on. You got to do better than that." "We're federal marshals." "That's cool. What'cha want?" "We got a warrant for your arrest." So I said, "Well, wait a minute. I got to put some clothes on." I went and got dressed and picked up the phone to call my lawyer and let him know what was going on.

I'd left the door open, but I had a chain across it. I left it open so they could see inside and see that I wasn't preparing for no shoot-out with 'em or nothing like that. But they decided they wanted to play cowboy and they came trying to kick the door down. I told them to stop kicking on the door. Kunstler wasn't in his New York office, but his brother who's also a lawyer was there, and he told me that it would be best to go ahead with 'em.

I took the chain off the door and all eight of 'em come rushing in, waving their guns all over the place. I sat down in a chair. "O.K., what'cha want?" I asked 'em. "We got a warrant for your arrest." I said, "Let me see it." They said it was an outstanding warrant, which meant that they didn't have it, but it was being drawn up. So I asked them, "What's the charges?" They didn't even know. Well, I started to argue with 'em but I decided that it was just too many folks there for me to argue with. But then they started looking through the house and I stopped 'em. "You got a search warrant?" One of 'em said, "You got any guns in here?" I said, "No." What kind of a fool he think I am? If I did have some guns there, I wasn't going to tell him of all people. They took me on down to the federal building and booked me. The next day I went on down to New Orleans where the warrant had been issued. The judge said I was guilty of violating bond and he set a new bond on me of $50,000.

During a recess in the hearing, before the judge set new bond, I was out in the corridor talking to some Black students who had come down to the court. This ol' negro FBI agent come walking up to me. The dude had testified against me in court, saying he had heard me speak out in California so I recognized him. Before he could get a word out of his mouth, I said to him, "I hope your children don't grow up to be a Tom like you are." I get back in court and I see this traitor on the stand telling the judge that I'd threatened his life. So the judge charged me with threatening an FBI agent and set $50,000 on that charge.

So now I had $100,000 bond on me and the judge in Virginia decided he had to get in his kicks, too. So he forfeited the bond he'd already set on me, which had been posted, and ordered that once I got out of jail in Louisiana, he wanted to see me again. This was clearly illegal as I didn't even have any charges against me in Virginia. But they had my ass and knew it and weren't about to cut me no slack.

They took me back to New Orleans where I was to remain in jail until SNCC could raise the $100,000 to get me out. This was a ridiculous bond. There was a woman in New York, Alice Crimmins, who was convicted of murdering her daughter, and they let her out on $25,000 bond, which meant that all she had to put up was $2,500 cash. I was being held on $100,000 cash and I hadn't killed nobody, robbed no bank or done anything. It was obvious that that was not bond. That was ransom!

When I got back to New Orleans I decided to go on a hunger strike. I figured that I had to draw the line. You have to resist whatever is done to you and I had no other weapon in jail except to not eat. I had to resist them muthafuckas somehow. I may have been in their jail, but I wasn't going to accept it. So that Black people would understand, I wrote my second Letter from Jail:

February 21, 1968

Being a man is the continuing battle of one's life and one loses a bit of manhood with every stale compromise to the authority of any power in which one does not believe.

No slave should die a natural death. There is a point where caution ends and cowardice begins.

For every day I am imprisoned, I will refuse both food and water.

My hunger is for the liberation of my people.

My thirst is for the ending of oppression.

I am a political prisoner, jailed for my beliefs (that Black people must be free). The government has taken a position true to its fascist nature—those they cannot convert, they must silence. This government has become the enemy of mankind.

This can no longer alter our path to freedom. For our people, death has been the only known exit from slavery and oppression. We must open others.

Our will to live must no longer supersede our will to fight, for our fighting will determine if our race shall live. To desire freedom is not enough. We must move from resistance to aggression, from revolt to revolution.

For every Orangeburg, there must be 10 Detroits.

For every Max Stanford and Huey Newton, there must be 10 racist cops.

And for every Black death there must be a Dien Bien Phu.

Brothers and sisters, as well as all oppressed people, you must prepare yourselves both mentally and physically, for the major confrontation is yet to come. You must fight. It is the people who in the final analysis make and determine history, not leaders or systems. The laws to govern you must be made by you.

May the deaths of '68 signal the beginning of the end of this country. I do what I must out of the love for my people. My will is to fight. Resistance is not enough. Aggression is the order of the day.

Note to america

America, if it takes my death to organize my people to revolt against you,
And to organize your jails to revolt against you,
And to organize your troops to revolt against you,
And to organize your children to revolt against you,
And to organize your God to revolt against you,
And to organize your poor to revolt against you,
And to organize your country to revolt against you,
And to organize Mankind to rejoice in your destruction and ruin,
Then, here is my Life!
But my Soul belongs to my people.
Lasima Tushinde Mbilashaka (We Shall Conquer Without a Doubt).

Yours in Revolution,
H. Rap Brown

SNCC mimeographed the letter and got it distributed. After I got out of jail, I learned that Julius Lester, a member of SNCC's Central Committee at that time, had read the letter at an anti-war rally at the U.N. and had been booed by the white people there. This was right after the Orangeburg Massacre and if whites disapproved of what I said in the letter, it showed me once again that John Brown was the only white man I could respect and he is dead. The Black Movement has no use for white liberals. We need revolutionaries. Revolutions can use revolutionaries.

After I had fasted eleven days I wrote another Letter:

March 2, 1968

The deaths and arrests of 1968 signal more than ever the resounding denial of human rights by this country. Murder and human bondage made justice the after-birth of america's immoral conception. True to the nature of its birth through murder and slavery, america's only offspring has been tyranny.

Who really violates the codes of justice? Justice upon which all "laws" should be fabricated. This country has shown that her "laws" are not based on justice; they are based on politics. There is no separation of "law" from politics. Political perspective and allegiance determine human rights. The courts are a tool of the political structure. America's judiciary system serves the political one. When justice serves the "law," then there is no law, no rights, no redress of grievance; only political and judicial intercourse. This government has made a mockery of its Constitution. Freedom shares my cell on Death Row.

Our only redress of grievance is through revolution. No government is worth more than humanity. Tyrants are to be made accountable for tyranny.

When the courts are no longer an instrument of or

116

for the people, the people must then become lawmakers and law enforcers.

If It Please the Court

Your country cheers for thee;
  My people are dying.
Giving my peers to thee;
  My people are dying.
My people tears to see;
  Our people are dying.
Your country tis of thee;
  Today you are dying.
Your country tears to see;
  No flag is flying.
My people cheers to see;
  We caused your dying.
My country tis of thee, sweet land of liberty . . .
Lasima Tushinde Mbilashaka
We Shall Conquer Without a Doubt

Yours in Revolution,
H. Rap Brown

A lot of Black people, even some in SNCC, wanted me to come off the hunger strike. They would send me messages saying that if I died, it would be just what "the man" wanted. I figured that if they didn't want me to die, they should get me out anyway they could. I was down there fighting with the only weapon I had, my life, and these folks wanted me to cop a plea. The authorities were very worried that I was going to die. I had them up tight. They figured on putting me in jail and if I was quiet, people would forget. But I fucked with 'em. I figured there wasn't no better place to die than in a united states jail. A lot of Black people, though, couldn't understand what I was doing.

117

Kunstler appealed the bond and eventually the $100,000 was knocked down to $30,000. The money was posted, but they still wouldn't let me go. I was in jail for a week and a half after the money was put up. I spent 43 days in that jail and fasted all 43.

When I was released, they took me to Virginia, where they put me in a concentration camp near Petersburg. My cell was underground. The window looked right out on top of the grass and the only thing else I could see was this large chimney of a furnace and this chimney was steady pumping black smoke.

I was in the camp and the judge wouldn't set bond. This was at the time that King was murdered and Black folks were burning down everything they could stick a match to, so I knew they weren't about to set bond and let me out. My lawyer appealed to every court he could and nobody would set bond. His next move was going to be to appeal to the Supreme Court. "Well," I said, "fuck that." I was tired because every night a guard would come around and shine a light in my eyes every hour. I was in a cell block by myself and between me and the outside there were five locked doors. So there wasn't any question about me going somewhere. I could only conclude that the dude shining the light in my eyes all night was simply trying to harass me. If he just wanted to make a bed check, he could see if I was there without throwing that light in my eyes. So I decided to waive extradition and go on back to Maryland. I knew that Baltimore had just gone up in smoke and I figured Maryland didn't hardly want to see me. So I fooled 'em and waived extradition.

The Virginia cops took me to the Maryland line and waiting for me there were 20 cops, the FBI, the Maryland State Attorney General, the Chief of Police from Cambridge and I don't know who else. I said, "Damn! They must think I'm Jack the Ripper or somebody." They put me in this unmarked car with five state trooper cars in front and three behind. And when we got to to the courthouse in Cambridge there were about 60 troopers lined up outside the courthouse. Meanwhile, they got me handcuffed and the handcuffs were handcuffed to my belt. I couldn't even have scratched.

They were scared shitless. All them pigs for me and the most dangerous weapon I had on me was my fingernails and they were cut short. But they were tomming worse than negro Toms. And you ain't seen no Toms until you see white folks tom. It was "Mr. Brown this" and "Mr. Brown the other." Yeah, them white folks tommed that day.

They took me down to be fingerprinted. Well, I wondered how many sets they needed, but I figured everybody had to have his own original. I don't know. Maybe they figured I'd changed my fingerprints between Virginia and there. Anyway the dude made one set and then he made another. Then he started to make a third. I said, "Wait a minute. How many you gon' make?" He said, "Five." I said, "Shit! I ain't making no five. I ain't never had to make no five sets of prints and you know I oughta know." I'd given fingerprints to everybody except Lyndon's mama. I told the dude, "Look-a-here. I'll give you three." So he took one more and I said, "Where's the stuff to clean up with?" He gave it to me and while I was cleaning up I heard somebody in the next room ask him if he'd gotten all five sets of prints. He said, "Oh—No. He said his fingers was sore."

After a little while, Kunstler showed up with the bond money. The bondsman came in and he was scared, pleading with me not to jump bond. The funny thing was that the state of Maryland got the bondsman. I'm on the white list and no bondsman across the country will post bond for me.

Maryland was so anxious to get rid of me that they went and got a bondsman themselves. Hell, if we hadn't had the money, I bet Agnew would've put it up himself.

So after almost two and a half months in jail for the crime of thinking and talking, I was out. But they hadn't silenced me. They'd taken me off the street, but I hadn't been silenced. They just gave me another forum. I talked to the brothers in jail, who are more political than the people on the streets. These are brothers who have no doubts as to what needs to be done.

The only reason that I'm willing to go before the racist courts is that it's an educational process for Black people. Black people should learn from my experiences. Every Black man shouldn't have to go before a judge to know what I'm experiencing. I was glad in Louisiana because the courtroom was filled with Black people, young Black brothers and sisters, every day. And they learned, because legally we beat the government on the first day. We made a motion to have this racist judge, "Mitch the Bitch," dismissed from the case because of prejudicial statements he made against me during some of the bond hearings we had before. The motion was made to him and he said, "Yeah, I'm prejudiced against him, but I'm not gonna dismiss myself."

The news media tries to project me as an enemy not only to the system, but to my people, and the high bail that has been set on me every time I've been arrested proves this. I'm a crazy, dangerous nigger, who hates white folks, according to the media. The news media is one of the greatest enemies to Black people. It is controlled by the ruling classes and is used to articulate their point of view. Every day the news media says, "The united states killed 2,000 Vietcong!" Hell, if you can count, it's obvious that there can't be no more Vietcong because the united states been killing them every day by the thousands for four years now. So it's

120

obvious that somebody's lying somewhere. But negroes got more confidence in Huntley and Brinkley than Catholics got in the Pope.

The media claims that I teach hate. Hate, like love, is a feeling. How can you teach a feeling? If Black people hate white people it's not because of me, it's because of what white people do to Black people. If hate can be taught, ain't no better teacher than white people themselves. I hate oppression. I am anti anybody who is anti-Black. Now if that includes most white people in america, it ain't my fault. That's just the way the bones break. I don't care whether or not white people hate me. It's not essential that a man love you to live. But "the man" has to respect you.

I believe that america loves the negro, though. It loves for him to do its work, loves for him to stay down under its foot. But america does not respect negroes; negroes don't respect themselves.

America is always playing her game, though. Turning anything and everything around to suit its own purposes. When Jews talk about what the Germans did to them, that's history and everybody agrees that it's history. But as soon as Black people begin to raise the question of what white folks have done to them and what white folks do to them daily, they say that it's hate. But you also got negro people walking around talking about Rap Brown and Carmichael teaching hate. The brothers know that if you saw a white man slap your sister down, you'd react with hate. It's not because anybody told you to hate the white man who slapped your sister, it's because you're supposed to hate a muthafucka who treats you worse than he treats his dog. The brothers knew all along that they didn't dig slavery.

Each individual Black person decides for himself whether or not he hates all whites. Racism in reverse is charged when Blacks don't profess their undying love for whites. But racism

the black side of American history.

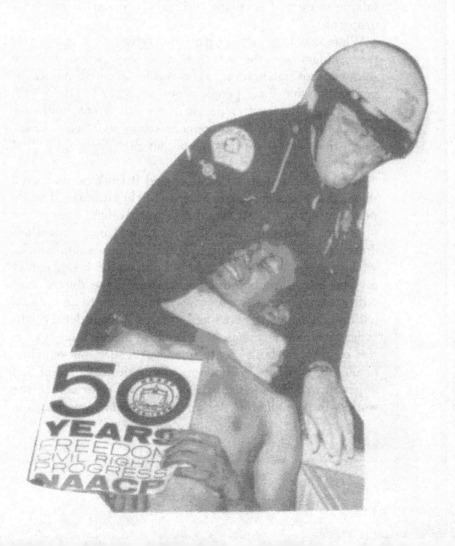

is based upon the concept of racial superiority, which Blacks have not yet alluded to. The Black Movement has never pushed the doctrine of racial superiority. But what upsets the media is that we don't say we love all white people. White folks get up tight if the first words a Black person say don't deal with love. That's their problem. If they haven't been oppressing Black people then they ain't got nothing to feel bad about. If they're fighting to destroy this racist country, then they know that what I'm saying about oppression does not apply to them. And they also know that I'm not talking to them. I'm talking to Black people. They're eavesdropping.

White people got hung up on integration. Segregation was the problem and the elimination of segregation was the solution, not integration. It was the unequal nature of segregation that Black people protested against in the South, not segregation itself. Separate but equal is cool with me. What's the big kick about going to school with white folks? Them that want to do that should have the chance. But that ain't no solution.

Racism stems from an attitude and it can't be destroyed under the capitalist system. You can't fight attitudes. If white people want to address themselves to that, fine. They're the ones with the attitude, but the Black Movement cannot address itself to attitudes. Fuck attitudes. Fuck a muthafucka who hates me, because if I ever get him on the wrong end of my gun he's in trouble. But Black people have always dealt with attitudes and attitudes always boil down to an individual thing. Change the laws and enforce 'em and let the attitudes take care of themselves. Because most of the laws in this country are built on attitudes, not justice, not equality, revolution is necessary. Racism, capitalism, colonialism and imperialism dominate the lives of people of color around the world—the people of Africa, Asia, Latin America, the

124

colonized minorities who live inside the united states. Fanon says of racism, "It stares one in the face for it so happens that it belongs in a characteristic whole: that of the shameless exploitation of one group of men by another which has reached a higher stage of technical development. That is why military and economic oppression generally precedes, makes possible, and legitimatizes racism. The habit of considering racism as a mental quirk, as a psychological flaw, must be abandoned." Racism does not operate as an individual force, it is an integral part of colonial oppression. We must understand that all colonized people are victims of racism and exploitation, but that all exploited people are not colonized. For instance, inside the united states we see some whites who are oppressed and who are exploited, but they do not suffer from the racism which is forced upon Blacks by whites, they in fact form a part of the colonizing race. Some of the most racist whites are the oppressed whites.

Our job is not to convert whites. If whites are dedicated to revolution then they can be used in the struggle. However, if they impede the struggle and are proven to be a problem then it is up to us to deal with them as with all problems. Our job now is to project what should be our common goal—the destruction of a system that makes slavery profitable.

Now there're a lot of people who say that the way you change laws is to destroy the power structure. I say you got to go beyond that. If you destroy the power structure, it can always be replaced by another power structure, whether it's white or Black. The power structure serves the system and the system is the thing which demands exploitation of people. You have to destroy the system. You can destroy the power structure and leave the system intact. But if you get the system, you got the power structure. That's the job which confronts us.

However we may twist our words and regardless of our

personal, subjective feelings—the truth of the matter is that we cannot end racism, capitalism, colonialism and imperialism until the reins of state power are in the hands of those people who understand that the wealth, the total wealth of any country and the world, belongs equally to all people. Societies and countries based on the profit motive will never insure a new humanism or eliminate poverty and racism. However we may twist our words and regardless of our personal feelings—the stark reality remains that the power necessary to end racism, colonialism, capitalism and imperialism will only come through long, protracted, bloody, brutal and violent wars with our oppressors.

Liberation movements must be based upon political principles that give meaning and substance to the struggle of the masses of people, and it is this struggle that advances the creation of a people's ideology. Liberation movements from the very beginning must be dedicated to principles that speak to the needs of the poor and oppressed, or must evolve into this type of movement with these principles while the fighting is going on, for it is not evident that those who fight will assume power and implement decisions that appropriate the wealth of countries for all people. Rather to the contrary: the absence of these revolutionary political principles relates to the fact that some new rulers have settled for a new flag, a new style of dress, a seat in the UN, and/or accommodation with former colonial powers. A negotiated independence.

We must draw from all ideologies those principles which benefit the majority of mankind. We cannot limit ourselves to just one concept or ideology that was relevant in some other revolution. As Debray points out, and correctly so, in his book *Revolution Within the Revolution*: "Revolutions cannot be imported nor exported." Certain changes have made even some of the most advanced ideologies obsolete.

128

For example, socialism as it exists today *ideologically* may be impractical for certain oppressed peoples. But the political principles of socialism certainly have validity. This is why in Cuba and other liberated countries the principles of socialism are being incorporated into the ideologies of these countries. This again goes back to Fanon's observation that we must extend the Marxian analysis when we view colonialism. It is the political principles that make the ideology; as these principles are refined through struggle an ideology is created.

Many people have had these principles (principles that speak to the needs of the mass of humanity) in mind as they were waging a struggle for independence, but having failed to win independence by defeating the enemy through armed struggle, it was necessary for them to negotiate with the colonial powers. In this process of negotiation, the colonial powers granted political autonomy but maintained economic influence, control and investments. The mere act of negotiating freedom means that the control necessary to appropriate the entire wealth of the country did not fall to the new leaders. We should have learned by now from history that the process of negotiating freedom and not winning it by armed struggle has built-in limitations. We must be prepared to fight to the death to destroy this system known as capitalism, for it is this system that oppresses the majority of mankind.

Vanguard groups must begin to reevaluate politics. What is known as politics in this country is meaningless. People have been told that politics means the Democratic and Republican parties; federal, state and local government; the vote. History shows that politics as it is defined by america is undesirable and dangerous to Black people, for the politics of capitalism has always been human oppression and exploitation. We must begin to relate to the politics of revo-

129

lution. Chairman Mao says, "Politics is war without bloodshed and war is an extension of politics." Every action that we are involved in is political, whether it is religious, artistic, cultural, athletic, governmental, educational, economic or personal. There is no separation between church and state, art and politics, or politics and individual beliefs. Everything is inherently political. The only division occurs around the question of whose political interest one will serve.

This country has always used negroes as a political tool against Blacks. Without a common Black political doctrine, america will use (and is using) Blacks against Blacks. Blackness must be political in our behalf. Individuals can no longer be immune to public political criticism because they are "Black and proud." There must be revolutionary political criticism of counter-revolutionary positions and acts. Some individuals who gain popularity in Black america are later used as tools by white america. In most cases, white political interest comes as a result of the existing popularity of the Black individuals. Understand, popularity does not reflect correctness. Blackness alone is not revolutionary.

If we examine Cleveland, Ohio, Gary, Indiana, Washington, D.C., and many other areas populated predominately by Blacks we can see a tactic being used that has often been tried in Africa, Vietnam and other oppressed countries. It is called neo-colonialism. In other words, when white structures and institutions are threatened whites protect their economic and political interests and maintain control by using members of the oppressed people as their spokesmen. They set up puppet governments headed by individuals with white interests in mind. These people oppress their own kind for their personal gain. These puppet leaders are as dangerous as those whom they represent. Remember, it was Jews who began to remove other Jews for Hitler. Even if the flunky's interest is sincere, he is powerless against the

130

system. Individuals do not mandate the action of the system; rather, the system demands certain actions of them. The only constructive thing a Black mayor can do is to organize Blacks to destroy the system that oppresses Black people. We must never permit anyone, white or Black, to destroy with impunity the product of a single drop of the blood and sweat of our people.

White folks realize now that they can concede Blackness and still exercise control. This country says, "Yes, you may be Black; but, you must be american," which means we are as responsible for oppression as whites. This country says, "Yeah, you may have Black heroes; but, we must approve of them." So, they publicize negroes who have been beneficial to this country. The tactic of co-opting is being used to its fullest. White folks will co-opt dog shit if it's to their advantage. Today, niggers are tomming and don't even know they're tomming. We must say as Fidel Castro says, "No liberalism whatsoever! No softening whatsoever! A revolutionary people, a political people—a strong people—this is what is needed throughout these years. . . . What do the dangers or the sacrifices of a man or of a nation matter when the destiny of humanity is at stake?"

12

In the course of a struggle for liberation, there will be individuals who will dedicate themselves and contribute all their energies. Their only lasting reward must be victory. However, acknowledgement can precede victory. In comparison to their contributions, acknowledgement is no more than a small reward.

History is always unkind to those who really make revolutions. This, my last speech in Detroit, is dedicated to those whom I feel have furthered the liberation struggle of Blacks. I only wish I could give more.

The following list is by no means complete, nor does it imply that these are the only revolutionary people I've worked with. After the first name this list has no designed order. The first individual has consistently committed himself totally and completely to the struggle: Bob Smith, more so than any other individual, symbolizes revolutionary spirit and attitude. His contributions are immeasurable; Willie Ricks, Faye Bellemy, Matthew Jackson, Theophalus Smith, Ralph Featherstone, Johnnie Jackson, Julius Lester, James Forman, Brother Crook. This is just a partial list of those who have contributed greatly. For these individuals that are listed and for those others that have given—given even in some cases their lives—I say the words of the Black poet Georgia Douglas Johnson:

My pathway lies through worse than death;
I meet the hours with bated breath,
My red blood boils, my pulses thrill,
I live life running up a hill.

133

Ah, No, I need no paltry play
Of make-shift tilts for holiday
For I was born against the tide
And will conquer that denied.

I shun no hardship, fear no foe;
The future calls and I must go:
I charge the line and dare the spheres
As I go fighting down the years.

To these individuals, I say, *LASIMA TUSHINDE MBILA-SHAKA* (We Shall Conquer Without a Doubt).

Brothers and Sisters:
I've just seen the battlefield; you did a thorough job.
There was a town called Motown; now it ain't no town.
They used to call it Detroit, now they call it Destroyed. I
hear ain't nothing left, but Motown sound. And if they don't
come around, you gon' burn them down. They say ain't no-
body left but Smokey and that's a "Miracle."
Langston Hughes wrote a poem called, "A Dream De-
ferred." This poem is for the benefit of those who pretend
not to understand what has occurred (not only here but
throughout this corrupt country). He raises the question:

What happens to a dream deferred?
Does it dry up like a raisin in the sun
or does it fester like a sore
and then run
or does it sag like a heavy load
or does it explode?

This poem was unanswered until Watts, Detroit, Newark,
Plainfield, Atlanta and every other city that has experienced

134

and felt the Black fire. Our dream is one of liberation, a right of self-determination, a dream of denied freedom; no more, no less. Our fire says we are no longer dreaming of freedom, we are exercising our rights to be free (at the expense of anybody who gets in our way). You see, freedom is absolute. You're either free or you're a slave. There is nothing in between freedom and slavery. There's no such thing as second-class citizens. That's like telling me you can be a little bit pregnant. Freedom is as absolute as truth. You're either lying or telling the truth. We were born free. We must exercise our right to be free.

Today I will talk about two things—colonialism and revolution. In other words, sickness and cure. The united states redefined colonialism. It not only went to Africa and exploited the land and its people; it brought Black people here and continues its exploitation; and it drove the native American Indians by murder and wholesale genocide onto reservations (and now this is romanticized on t.v. as cowboys and Indians). America is the ultimate denial of the theory of man's continuous evolution. This country represents everything that humans have suffered from, their every affliction. The very fact that a place like this can exist appals most of mankind. This country is the world's slop jar. America's very existence offends me. For Black people it is not a question of leaving or separating—given our historical experiences, we know better than anyone that the animal that is america must be destroyed. Through capitalism, this country establishes colonies; but, not colonies in the old sense, but like franchises. The Philippines, Venezuela, Vietnam, Puerto Rico and other countries are to the united states what dope is to Harlem; bloods use it, but the Mafia owns it. It just goes to show you, you give the cracker an inch, he wants a yard, give him a yard, and he'll BURN A CROSS ON IT, every time. There is no difference between Harlem and Puerto Rico, or

Harlem and Vietnam, except that in Vietnam people are fighting for their liberation. (That is, armed struggle.)

Let's examine that war in Vietnam. My position, on that war, is that Black folks ain't got no business shooting other Black folks for white folks. If we must fight, then our war is here at home. We can't let white folks decide for us who our enemy is. We must decide who our enemy is and how to deal with him. Black cats must say that if Lynch'em Burn Johnson can stay here and keep the Vietcong off Ladybird, then we can stay here and keep the crackers off our women. We must refuse to participate in the war of genocide against people of color: a war that also commits genocide against us. Black men are being used on the front lines at a disproportionate rate. Forty-five percent of the casualties are Black. That's genocide! We cannot let our Black brothers fight in Vietnam because we need them here to fight with us. If we can die defending our motherland, we can die defending our mothers. It is the Black man's will to be free that has made him fight for this country, not his love. This same will to be free will make him fight this country. The army is to kill people. We have to decide if we will be killers; when we decide, we have to decide who we are going to kill, and when.

We are the greatest victims of colonial rule. We are exposed to this country's strongest institutions every day. We find that what is called "education" is not education at all. What it is, is white nationalist propaganda. Black people are made to hate themselves. I saw a brother on the corner once, trying to figure out what was wrong with his skin— it didn't match his flesh-colored bandaid.

Media is used against us in total. The W.P.P. (white power people, or the white power press, or white people's power—take your choice) all victimize Blacks. The rebellion's aftermath brought demands in the white press not for the resolution of historic grievances of oppressed Blacks but for the guillotining of Carmichael or myself. The negro press is no better. They wait for white folks to tell them what to say. The tactic of media is to make you an enemy of the people. Enemies of the people are always vulnerable. The reason Malcolm could be killed and Black folks didn't revolt is that the press had made Malcolm an enemy of the people. More negroes were scared of Malcolm than whites. The reason they could give Muhammad Ali the maximum sentence and fine was because the press had made him an enemy of the people. The reason Adam Powell could be politically lynched and Black folks didn't revolt, was because Adam had been made an enemy of the people. Negroes believe anything the press says.

Anything you don't control can be used as a weapon against you. Education is used as a weapon against us. News media is used as a weapon against us. Athletics. We dominate in athletics, but we don't control them. Therefore the negro athlete is used as a weapon against us. This country realizes that the athlete has an image in our community. So they get some ol' bootlicking, shuffling, money-mad negro, who can run or jump, and they tell him, "Go control your people. If we can't control athletes, we can sure cripple 'em." Brothers ought to break him up so bad, until he'll have to die to get well. The same thing goes for entertainers. Teach them that if they can't say the right thing, then don't say nothing.

Another thing that is used effectively against Blacks is the court system. There is no justice in this country for Black people. Justice is a joke, and it stinks of hypocrisy. Lyndon Johnson is Hitler's illegitimate child and J. Edgar Hoover is his half-sister. Justice means "just-us-white-folks." There is no redress of grievance for Blacks in this country. When the government becomes the lawbreaker, people must become law enforcers. What happened at the Algiers Motel must not

137

be allowed to be repeated. The tribunal to be held must be made legal by the people. If the murderers are found guilty, and they should be, the brothers should carry out the execution.

When we begin to put all of these things together, we begin to understand what america is doing. Genocide can be seen in the mass removal of Blacks from the streets, by placing them in jails. Yes, the courts conspire to commit genocide. Black people are in the majority in most jails in this country. Concentration camps have been established and maintained throughout this country. They were established as a result of the McCarran Act of 1950. There is a book called Concentration Camps, U.S.A. that's written by Charles R. Allen—who is white. (I say this because it usually bridges the credibility gap; you don't believe what Black folks say but you believe white folks.) It is in your interest that you read it, because your not knowing what's going to happen doesn't make it any the less true. Me and Carmichael can't fill all them camps. They must be planning on taking somebody else. This country is waging a genocidal war against people of color; domestic and foreign. This is a country that pays white farmers for not growing food and dumps surplus food in the ocean. Birth control, as it's practiced by governmental programs dealing with the masses of poor, can't be called anything else but an attempt at genocide. Birth control should be an individual decision. It should not be forced by a government.

Some of you are probably saying america wouldn't do that kind of thing. Negroes like to believe that they are something special to this country. Well, let's examine america's history. The American Indian—total genocide. And "the man" shows it to you on t.v. The Japanese—america dropped the bomb on Japan and not on Germany, not because they didn't have the bomb, but because the Japanese are yellow.

When this country fought Germany, the German-Americans were not put in concentration camps; however, when they fought Japan, Japanese-Americans were put into concentration camps, in this country. The Vietnamese and Latin Americans—america says that she's in their countries to stop communist aggression. America has never moved to stop communist aggression in white countries by utilizing antipersonnel bombs and napalm; in Poland, Hungary, Czechoslovakia, she uses RADIO FREE EUROPE; never weapons of destruction. It is important to note here that all the countries with people of color are the ones militarily attacked by america. So why should we be immune to her racism? We experience it every day. We were brought here to do work, there is no more work. Machines do the jobs we used to do. The Attorney General made a statement a few weeks ago; it was interesting in this respect; he said, "Within 20 years the entire population of this country will be a leisure class, with the exception of ten percent of that population, because of automation and cybernation." Then when we look to see who they are training for those jobs, we find that they are training whites. So that lets me know that this country no longer needs Black people. America has a surplus of niggers. She then legitimatizes her program of genocide, by implanting into the minds of whites, and negroes, the idea that Blacks don't do anything but "riot and get on welfare." We put america on notice; IF WHITE FOLKS WANT TO PLAY NAZIS, BLACK FOLKS AIN'T GOING TO PLAY JEWS.

We have not made any progress since we have been in this country. We are still slaves! Concessions are not to be confused with progress. Whites have made concessions only out of political necessity. This country only loosens its hold on Black people to get a better grip. Whites and negroes talk of progress, and point to Thurgood Marshall. He is a con-

cession; white folks put him there, and can remove him when they get ready. James O. Eastland, a red-neck camel-breath moldy old cracker from Mississippi, subjected Thurgood to a level of questioning that was unheard of before. What he was really saying was, "You might be the top nigger in the country, but you are still a nigger to me." They gave negroes an astronaut; but, I bet they lose that nigger in space. [Note: He was killed in a jet crash while landing.] *We have not made any progress. Negroes go for anything white folks tell them or sell them.*

If "the man" wanted to he could tell Black folks, "Bring me all the rocks you can find, and for every rock you bring, I will give you a million dollars." Bloods would bring rocks for days, little rocks, big rocks, rocks nobody knew existed. And, when the man got all the rocks, he'd tell Black folks, "We're using rocks for money." Ask the South what the North did after the civil war. This country operates on an annual budget of 800 billion dollars. These dollars are supposedly backed by gold. The International Monetary System is also based on gold. This means that foreign countries can demand gold for america's paper dollars. France is now demanding payment in gold; america's foreign debt exceeds her quantity of gold. Relying upon one of its old tactics, america changed the rules. Through pressure from this country, the International Monetary System changed from gold to what is called paper gold. As the Chairman says, "Power comes from the barrel of a gun." Freedom is not for sale. Freedom can only be bought with revolution.

There must be a re-evaluation of politics. What is considered politics in this country is meaningless to Black people. Politics, as defined by the geographical and influential boundaries of this country, is irrelevant to masses of people. The vote is used as a tool of oppression. Camus raises a very good point. He says, "What better way to enslave a man,

140

than give him the vote and call him free." In other words,
what does it profit a man to be able to vote, and not be able
to choose his candidates. Politics in this country is not bi-
partisan; politics is very partial—partial toward whites with
money. The only politics that should be relevant to us is the
politics of revolution.

Everything must relate to the struggle as a political form.
Culture must be political. Nationalism alone is not a political
doctrine. Nationalism has to be a part of a political doctrine.
Without vanguard political direction cultural movements
bring economic and/or political liberalism, not revolution.
We must move to define the difference between political
nationalism and cultural nationalism. We must move from
Black awareness to revolutionary motion. "To be Black is
necessary but not sufficient." Every negro is a potential
traitor; and every Black man is only a potential revolutionary
—with emphasis on potential. To be Black is not to be revo-
lutionary. When you begin to stress culture without politics,
people can become so hooked up in the beauty of themselves
that they have no desire to fight. It becomes ego-gratifying
just to be Black. Vanguard groups can't afford to go around
stressing culture without politics, the real test now is prep-
aration for, and initiation of, struggle. Write me a novel
about how to infiltrate the FBI and destroy it. Write me
poems that say more than that you are Black and beautiful.
Perform dances with guns to legitimatize guns as a weapon
of struggle. If you examine any country that has undergone
successful revolution, you will find that the cultural revolu-
tion has never come before actual armed confrontation,
never before a contest for power was waged.

[Note: Today we see the Black world divided on the question of ideology. Throughout Africa the lack of common
political motion divides people against people and insures

opportunism by certain leaders. Inside the united states this is a paramount problem where groups of Blacks are struggling in various ways for liberation. This struggle is being checked through the lack of a common political objective. The concept of Black Power, for instance, has been diluted and prostituted to the point where even the most conservative negroes are now for Black Power. "Whitey" Young, dictator of the urban league, preaches for Black pride and acclaims that Black Power is attainable through Black capitalism. A lot of cats said the blood is coming home, but look again, he's still following his master. Floyd McKissick, former director of CORE, who once argued for Black Power maintains that Black people need Black capitalism. The united states government is in the process of giving tax incentives to those who start Black businesses and invest in Black areas; and the unlimited Ford Foundation, which has been trying to buy up the Movement for years, and which funds everything from Black television programs to experiments in school decentralization, has recently declared that it will place some of its investment portfolio in developing Black capitalism. All Black folks considering revolutionary work must be aware of these pitfalls. We must study how revolutions are aborted, how independence movements are stifled, how people are cheated of the fruits of their efforts, how the foot soldier or the Mau Mau gets betrayed by the bourgeois nationalist—these are things that all revolutionaries must understand. *(January, 1969)*]

At this stage of struggle the greatest danger comes from within. It has become profitable, fashionable and even necessary to be Black. In that order. Militancy is second to Blackness. However, to be militant is not to be revolutionary. Upon close examination, I find the thrust of most militancy is toward reform, not revolution. A militant in this case is one who never stops talking. Militants will bust their balls, campaigning to get some cracker elected. Black militants grow naturals to appear on t.v. as cops shooting blacks for this country. There is not one negro on t.v. that has a politically meaningful role: I Spy is the logical extension of The Lone Ranger; *my man is just Tonto. In* Mission Impossible, *the brother is a humanoid, a professional mechanic for the CIA. All of these shows play against Black people; they might help individuals but never the masses. They are designed to keep Blacks militantly happy. Black militants talk about revolution while seriously programming white people for money. This is the new hustle. Niggers running around with naturals on their heads and nothing on their minds. Some of the biggest and the prettiest naturals belong to the police. Black militant disc-jockies, militantly trying to convince white people they got "blue-eyed soul." Militant negro magazines advising Blacks on which white man to vote for.*

Militancy, too, must be political. We must begin to see ours as the struggle of oppressed people. We are not the only oppressed people in this country. We are a vanguard force in the revolution because we have been the most dispossessed. The Mexican-American, the Puerto Rican, the American Indian, Japanese-American, poor whites; all these groups have reason to fight. Repression will force them to fight. However, it is doubtful that poor whites can overcome racism. We hold the key to liberation around the world. The freedom of people around the world depends upon what we do. This is true, because this country is the chief oppressor around the world. If we view this country as an octopus, then we see that her tentacles stretch around the globe. Like in Vietnam, Africa, Latin America. . . . If these countries cut off a tentacle, it can be replaced. But we got his eye; we live in the belly of the monster. So it's up to us to destroy its brain. When we do this not only will Africa be free but all people oppressed by "the man." It is because of america's

143

racism and greed that Black people and people of color around the world are oppressed.

The question of violence has been cleared up. This country was born of violence. Violence is as american as cherry pie. Black people have always been violent, but our violence has always been directed toward each other. If nonviolence is to be practiced, then it should be practiced in our community and end there. Violence is a necessary part of revolutionary struggle. Nonviolence as it is advocated by negroes is merely a preparation for genocide. Some negroes are so sold on nonviolence that if they received a letter from the White House saying to report to concentration camps, they would not hesitate. They'd be there on time! If we examine what happened to the Jews, we find that it was not the Germans who first began to remove Jews. It was other Jews! We must be prepared to fight anyone who threatens our survival. Black and white. The rebellions taught Blacks the value of retaliatory violence. The most successful rebellion was held in Plainfield. It was successful in the sense that white violence was minimized. The only death that occurred in Plainfield was that of a white racist cop. We know how sensitive america is about the killing of policemen—especially white policemen. But both National Guardsmen and local police were afraid to shoot up the Black community because the brothers had just stolen two crates of guns. Each one of these guns would shoot seven times before you load it, which makes it hard to hold it; eight times fore you cock it, and it takes a man to stop it. The very fact that white folks fear guns shows the value in being armed. Power, indeed, must come from the barrel of a gun.

We can no longer allow threats of death to immobilize us. Death is no stranger to Black folks. We've been dying ever since we got here. To all the brothers and sisters who are here, ours may be to do and die, but for the little brothers *and sisters, theirs should be but the reason why. This country has delivered an ultimatum to Black people; america says to Blacks: you either fight to live or you will live to die. I say to america, Fuck It! Freedom or Death.*

Power to the People.